Introduction to Programmatic Advertising

SECOND EDITION

Dominik Kosorin

Introduction to Programmatic Advertising
by Dominik Kosorin

Copyright © 2022 Dominik Kosorin. All rights reserved.
Published by Dominik Kosorin in Prague.
Cover and interior design by Anezka Hruba Ciglerova.
June 2022: Second Edition.

ISBN: 978-80-907138-6-4

For Zuzana, Samuel, and David

CONTENTS

Acknowledgments	11
Introduction	12
Book overview	15

Chapter 1
Basic Technologies — 18

Cookies	19
First-party vs. Third-party cookies	20
Practical applications of cookies	21
Cookies in the programmatic ecosystem	23
Tracking pixels and scripts	28
Web browsers	30
HTML	31
Banner ads	32
Ad servers	34

Chapter 2
Programmatic Advertising Ecosystem — 35

Buy side	37
Advertisers	37
Demand side platforms	39
Sell side	42
Publishers	42
Supply side platforms	45
Other ecosystem participants	47
Ad verification vendors	47
Consent management platform vendors	48
Identity providers and initiatives	48
Ad servers	49

Industry bodies	49
Interactive Advertising Bureau	50
Trustworthy Accountability Group	51
Media Rating Council	51
Other industry bodies and regulators	52

Chapter 3
Programmatic Standards — 53

Programmatic transaction types	53
Auction-based transaction types	55
Fixed price transaction types	57
Trading standards	58
OpenRTB	59
OpenDirect	64
Other standards	65
First-price auction	66

Chapter 4
Trading in Practice — 67

Buy side	67
Buying algorithms	67
Bid shading	69
Frequency capping	69
Measurement	70
Attribution	71
Supply-path optimization	73
Sell side	76
Yield management setup	76

Programmatic trading issues	80
Fraud	80
Viewability	83
Ad blocking	85

Chapter 5
Data — 87

Advertising data basics	88
Data sources	88
Data creation methods	94
Data categories	95
Data ownership	98
Advertising data ecosystem	102
Advertisers	103
Publishers	104
Closed advertising platforms	104
Data vendors and exchanges	105
Data Management Platforms and Customer Data Platforms	105
Data activation	106
Prospecting	107
Retargeting	114

Chapter 6
Identity — 119

Identity	119
Why is identity important?	120
Legacy identity ecosystem	121
Evolution of user identity	125

Chapter 7
Privacy — 132

Privacy regulation — 134
   General Data Protection Regulation — 135
   ePrivacy Directive and ePrivacy Regulation — 139
   California Consumer Privacy Act — 140
   California Online Privacy Protection Act — 141
   Children's Online Privacy Protection Act (COPPA) — 142

Self-regulation — 142
   Digital Advertising Alliance (DAA) Self-Regulatory Program — 143

Technology vendor initiatives — 144
   Browsers — 144
   Operating Systems — 145

Identity and Privacy — 146

Chapter 8
Emerging Media Channels — 149

Connected TV — 149
   Connected TV and programmatic trading — 153
   Current issues with connected TV — 154

Retail media — 157

Programmatic audio — 158

Programmatic out-of-home — 159

About the author — **163**
References — **164**

Acknowledgments

My wife Zuzana, who supports and encourages me through all my writing projects. Zuzana Neupauerova and Jakub Novotny, whose many valuable suggestions helped me make both the first and second editions of this book much better. Anezka Hruba Ciglerova, who designed the exquisite book cover and layout. Samuel and David, who inspire me with their smiles, energy, and curiosity.

Introduction

Advertising is and will continue to be programmatic. Just a few years ago, it was an exciting new trend that promised a marketing revolution. It is astounding to see how quickly this revolution transformed an entire industry, with no sign of slowing down. Soon, we will most likely stop differentiating programmatic advertising altogether, and just take for granted that all advertising happens largely in an automated fashion.

Why is this happening, and why at such a breakneck pace? The magic of programmatic advertising comes from a powerful combination of automation and data. With programmatic, each ad impression is bought and sold individually, in a very efficient automated trading ecosystem. Moreover, each transaction can potentially draw on a wealth of data to inform an optimal message or clearing price. For example, a phone retailer can reach out to a potential customer with the right model and message at the exact time they are in the market for a new smartphone. The answer is therefore simply unprecedented efficiency, particularly for advertisers. Higher efficiency means lower costs and higher return on investment, with a lot of potential still up for grabs.

As noted in the first edition of this book, it is data that elevates programmatic advertising to its game-changer status. And naturally it is indeed data that has recently become a highly contested territory. This battle is played out indirectly though, through privacy and identity changes and their impact on data access for individual players. The reason for this is simple. In programmatic, access to data directly translates into trading efficiency, and efficiency attracts advertising spend. Whoever controls data, or at least more of it than the competition, wins in this new advertising reality.

Of all the changes in programmatic advertising over the past several years, there are two that stand out in terms of their impact. Both are a direct response to user demand for more privacy, but each takes a different approach to delivering on it. First is the gradual deprecation of third-party cookies in web browsers. For an ecosystem built on third-party cookies and depending on them for interoperability and measurement, this is a huge challenge. User identity went from something that used to be taken for granted to a precious asset not all players will have access to. It remains to be seen how a new identity landscape takes shape, and whether the open programmatic ecosystem outlives this change. The second major development is the rise of user privacy protection and regulation. With the introduction of GDPR in the European Union or CCPA in California, first steps have been taken to give users visibility and control over their personal data. This is a positive trend, and we can expect further evolution of both legislation as well as technology to better deliver on its intent.

Beyond the rapid transformation in identity and privacy landscape, the past several years have brought other notable changes. Programmatic trading switched to a first-price auction as a response to the adoption of header bidding technology by publishers. This led to the emergence of new strategies and techniques, such as bid shading or supply-path optimization. Connected TV has risen to prominence as the new frontier for programmatic revolution, along with the fast-growing retail media. Overall, the ecosystem is consolidating and shifting from an open market with many cooperating and competing players to a collection of more or less closed "walled gardens".

This book aims to offer an introductory overview of the open programmatic advertising ecosystem with a focus on current issues. Just like the first edition, it was written primarily with people who are new to this world in mind. This includes people just entering the industry, students, academics, or anyone who would like to better understand how programmatic works. Some of the topics covered in this book, such as identity or privacy, could be also useful to seasoned professionals.

The book is intentionally relatively short, so it can be read over a weekend and provide a solid framework on which to build further knowledge. As noted previously, the scope of this book is mainly open programmatic ecosystem. Closed advertising systems (offered for example by Facebook, Google or Amazon) are not covered, as there are plenty of other resources available.

Book overview

Chapter one outlines the basic technologies enabling programmatic advertising such as cookies, pixels, web browsers, HTML, banner ads and ad servers. Having a firm grasp of the basics is key to understanding more advanced concepts further in the book.

Chapter two opens the door into the world of programmatic proper, introducing various players in the ecosystem. On the buy side, we will explore advertisers and demand-side platforms. On the sell side, publishers will be covered, along with supply-side platforms. This chapter also introduces data management platforms and customer data platforms, as well as data, fraud, privacy and viewability vendors. Finally, there's a brief overview of industry bodies and other regulators.

Chapter three delves into the standards of programmatic ad trading. We will look at auction based as well as fixed price transaction types, and the enabling OpenRTB and OpenDirect protocols and other industry norms.

Chapter four continues the thread from chapter three with an overview of selected practical considerations, techniques and issues present in programmatic ad trading. These include among others bidding strategies, bid shading, supply-path optimization, unified auction, fraud, ad blocking or measurement and attribution.

Chapter five is dedicated to data, a key ingredient giving programmatic advertising its power. In this chapter, we will cover some basics related to advertising data. These include an overview of sources, data creation methods and common categorizations. Then we'll briefly discuss the data ecosystem, before closing the chapter with a look at some data activation strategies such as prospecting or retargeting.

Chapter six explores the topic of identity, which is fundamental to programmatic advertising. First, the concept and its importance is laid out. Next, the legacy identity ecosystem based on third-party cookies is explained in depth, to be contrasted with alternative approaches such as first-party cookie-based identity or user authentication.

Chapter seven closely follows up the identity discussion with an overview of the state of user privacy protection. It covers government regulation such as GDPR or CCPA, as well as self-regulation and technology vendor initiatives. This chapter ends with a discussion of the relationship between privacy and identity, and implications for the industry.

Chapter eight focuses primarily on emerging programmatic channels, such as connected TV, retail media, digital audio or digital out-of-home.

Chapter 1
Basic Technologies

To make sense of programmatic advertising, you must first have a firm grasp of some very basic technologies which lie at its core. If you are completely new to digital advertising (term used interchangeably with online advertising), this chapter will throw you right into the deep end of online technology pool. Don't worry if something doesn't make sense right away, the programmatic ecosystem is complex, and the dots will eventually connect as you read the following chapters.

This chapter will give a quick overview of cookies & pixels, web browsers, HTML, banner ads and ad servers. Of course, this is just a selection of the most critical foundational bits common to all display advertising (not just programmatic), rather than an exhaustive technology overview. More advanced concepts and technologies will be explored in later chapters of this book. Without first understanding the basics though, the following chapters could become slightly confusing.

Cookies

Cookies are one of the key building blocks of programmatic advertising today, albeit their importance is steadily declining. Even as third-party cookies are quickly deprecated and new restrictions are placed on the use of first-party cookies, it is important to have a firm understanding of how they work. Since cookies have been the backbone of digital advertising for decades, their legacy will be long visible in the ecosystem.

A cookie is a small piece of data sent from a web server and stored in a web browser. Every time a web browser makes a request to a server, this data is sent back to the server along with the request. As the request is fulfilled, web server can update cookie in the browser as well.

Cookie data is stored in a text file, in key-value pairs. Every cookie has a **name** and **value** and can also contain one or several additional attributes such as **expiry date**. This data can be read only by the server domain which set it. For example, if a cookie was set by a server on the domain **publisherexample.com**, it cannot be read by a server on the **trackerexample.com** domain. Also, every browser manages its own cookies. This means that a single internet user might have multiple cookies from the same domain (e.g. in **Google Chrome** as well as **Mozilla Firefox**).

The reason cookies were invented and are very useful today is maintaining state of a browser session - keeping track of all the user activity related to a particular browser and domain. The HTTP protocol is stateless by design, which means that without cookies, a web server would treat every request as an isolated event. Cookies let the web server know that some requests are related and can provide additional information that is helpful when fulfilling them.

First-party vs. Third-party cookies

The difference between first- and third-party cookies is in the domain that created them. First-party cookies are set by a server on the same domain a user is directly visiting, while third-party cookies are set by a server on a domain user is not visiting directly. For example, if a user visits **publisherexample.com**, their browser might get a first-party cookie under **publisherexample.com** domain, and a third-party cookie under **trackerexample.com** domain. This is technically achieved by pulling content from various domains to build a webpage, allowing servers on these domains to set cookies. While the bulk of the text and images might come from a server on the **publisherexample.com** domain, **trackerexample.com** could for instance provide ads, comments plugin, or simply an invisible pixel for tracking purposes.

Third-party cookies have always been controversial from a privacy perspective, to the point where browsers decided to make them obsolete. If **trackerexample.com** can set and access cookies across many websites, they are able to track users (albeit anonymous) and collect their data as they browse. Such tracking often happens without user knowledge, let alone consent. This practice came under scrutiny from both regulators (with new restrictions on cookie use enacted under ePrivacy Directive and General Data Protection Regulation, discussed later in a chapter on privacy) as well as internet browsers. Third-party cookies are set to be finally phased out in 2023, when Google Chrome - the most popular browser - will join Safari, Firefox and Microsoft Edge and stop supporting them[1]. The demise of third-party cookies is an enormous change for programmatic advertising, as the entire ecosystem is built on them. Due to the gravity of its implications, this will be discussed in a separate chapter on identity.

Practical applications of cookies

First and foremost, cookies are commonly used as storage for user identity in web environment. When a user visits a page for the first time, the web server saves a cookie with a unique user ID in their browser. From this point on (until the cookie is deleted or expires), the server can identify all requests coming from the same user. This ability to hold user identity in a cookie lends itself to several common use cases.

Firstly, cookies enable website personalization. For example, users' language preferences, custom layout or content might be used to build each webpage on **publisherexample.com**, making the browsing experience more personal and enjoyable. An e-commerce platform could use purchase and browsing history to suggest products a user might be interested in.

Secondly, cookies help keep track of temporary user states. If the user has for instance logged in, their cookie is used to keep track of the logged-in state. A cookie might also be used to keep track of an online shopping basket – contents, quantities, timestamps etc. This data is typically saved in a database on the server (server-side), and cookie is used for matching data to a particular user. This way, the server knows the state of the shopping basket for this user and can display it properly with each page request.

Third, cookies enable better advertising - for users, marketers as well as publishers. Ads can be for instance tailored to users' likely preferences based on their behavioral data or have maximum daily frequency per user so as not to become a nuisance. Marketers benefit from precise targeting and attribution to increase efficiency and reach within their target group. And publishers get to serve relevant ads to their audience while making their inventory more valuable. Most of the advertising use cases are built on third-party cookies though, and it remains to be seen if they will get a suitable alternative once these are phased out.

Fourth, cookies are commonly used for tracking users and collecting their data. Third-party cookies in particular enable compilation of users' browsing history across domains, which can be both good and bad. A good use case for the programmatic industry is measurement and analytics of advertising campaigns, enabling real-time user level optimization and attribution. Another generally good use case is website personalization based on users' behavior, as discussed above. However, user tracking can be easily misused - fueling shady data businesses, pursuing aggressive retargeting strategies or putting user data at risk of leakage or abuse. Such practices are particularly controversial when they happen without user knowledge and consent.

Cookies in the programmatic ecosystem

From an industry perspective, cookies are predominantly used as storage of identity. As of 2022, the programmatic ecosystem relies on third-party cookies for this purpose, and each player tends to build their own identity graph. For example, a demand-side platform might set a cookie in users' browser every time it delivers ads, giving each browser a unique ID. This cookie would be set in the **dspexample.com** domain, and accessible only by a server on this domain as noted above. In addition, cookies are stored independently in each browser, so a typical user will have multiple IDs for each player/technology within the ecosystem. To overcome these issues, two techniques are commonly used - cookie syncing between ecosystem players, and cross-device ID resolution within each of the players' graphs.

COOKIE SYNCING

Cookie syncing (also called cookie matching) is a process of pairing cookies related to the same browser/user from one ad tech platform with those of another platform. This is necessary because, as noted above, cookies can be read only by the server domain (i.e. platform) which set them and no one else. Separate platforms (such as a DMP and DSP), each having set their own cookie, require cookie syncing to know the cookies are related to the same user and data transfer is therefore possible. Cookie syncing process between two platforms results in a match table (stored by either or both parties), which maps cookie IDs from one platform to cookie IDs from the other platform:

PLATFORM A'S USER ID	PLATFORM A'S COOKIE ID	PLATFORM B'S COOKIE ID
ABC	123	321
DEF	456	654
GHI	789	987

FIGURE 1: MATCH TABLE EXAMPLE

This is an example of how an actual sync happens using pixels:

1) User visits a website controlled by **platform A** (i.e. **platform A** can fire tags/pixels and set cookies). Synchronization pixel containing **platform A's** cookie ID will fire, targeted at **platform B**.

2) Upon receiving the sync request, **platform B** reads and saves **platform A's** cookie ID in a match table against its own cookie ID (if none exists, **platform B** can set a cookie at this time to create one).

3) **Platform B** redirects back to **platform A**, passing it **platform B's** cookie ID.

4) **Platform A** reads **platform B's** cookie ID and stores it in the match table against its own cookie ID.

INTRODUCTION TO PROGRAMMATIC ADVERTISING

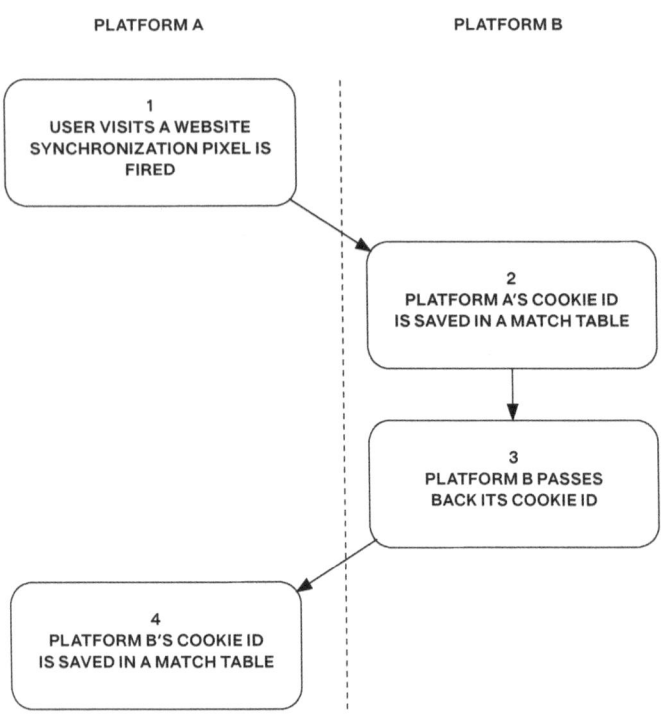

FIGURE 2: COOKIE SYNCHRONIZATION PROCESS

Now that **platform A** knows a user's ID used by **platform B** and vice versa, they can easily share data related to the same user. All that **platform B** needs to do is always attach its own ID whenever it transfers data to **platform A** (whether using tags, pixels, real-time server-to-server integration, batch processing, or even within bid requests in case of SSP/DSP communication).

CROSS-DEVICE ID RESOLUTION

Cross-device ID resolution is a technique for linking unique, independent IDs across different browsers and devices to the same user. A typical user would have many separate IDs even within one identity graph, due to two main reasons. Firstly cookies, the primary identity storage in the digital industry, are managed independently in each browser. To illustrate, a server on the domain **adtechnologyexample.com** would set a separate cookie with a unique **name=value** pair for each browser a user might employ to access the internet on the same device. So the same user could be identified as **user A** on Google Chrome and **user B** on Mozilla Firefox. Secondly, a typical user today would have multiple digital devices, such as work PC, mobile phone, smart TV, tablet, home laptop, smart speaker, fitness watch, etc. Each of these devices could be treated as one or multiple independent IDs (e.g. if multiple browsers are used on the device), further fragmenting user identity. Cross-device techniques are commonly used to overcome this challenge.

There are two basic approaches to cross-device ID resolution – probabilistic and deterministic. The deterministic approach takes advantage of a unique, persistent ID – such as a login, email address or a phone number. This guarantees very reliable cross-device user identification resistant to cookie deletion or third-party cookie blocking, but such an ID is not always available (generally this would require for a user to be constantly logged in). Probabilistic approach works differently – the method consists in analyzing vast quantities of data (such as device type, browser, operating system, IP address, user agent, location, etc.) to merge user profiles based on statistical probability. Probabilistic cross-device ID resolution can use deterministic connections as a base for learning. Although not as accurate, it can make up for it with an increased reach.

Tracking pixels and scripts

A tracking pixel (also known as tag) is a piece of code embedded in an email or a web page to track user activity. A tracking pixel is usually implemented as a tiny, invisible image (1x1, or one pixel), referenced through a single line of HTML code. Alternatively, JavaScript can be used for the same purpose, giving more tracking possibilities if JavaScript is enabled. Tracking pixels are commonly used for email marketing (to see if emails are opened, by whom and when), ad measurement, analytics or data collection.

Basic tracking pixel is essentially a vehicle for accessing cookies, enabling third-party servers to set and read cookies in users' browsers across many domains. When a web page is loaded, a tracking pixel will fire with request to a web server. This request can contain a lot of useful information – such as URL, time of the request, IP address, or whether any cookies from the web server have been previously set. Some of this information needs to be supplied to the pixel by the webpage though – for example, a simple pixel doesn't by itself know on which URL it is fired. However, it can contain a macro which can ingest page URL if offered by the web page. An alternative approach is to create a custom pixel for each URL, to differentiate on which URL the pixel is fired. Either way, information gathered by tracking pixels is logged, and the server can set cookies.

Beyond the typical implementations noted above, any external content on a website can serve as a tracking pixel – including banner ads, social media buttons or various plugins. For publishers, it is therefore extremely important to know which tracking pixels are allowed on their web sites, to protect their valuable data and user privacy.

To manage tracking pixels and more complex scripts on a web site efficiently, publishers often implement a tag management system (such as Google Tag Manager or Adobe's Dynamic Tag Management). Such systems offer a simple user interface and require only initial implementation by the IT department. After that, tracking pixels can be easily added or removed by the responsible team (such as digital marketing).

Web browsers

A web browser is an application used for accessing websites. For instance, when a user requests a web page from the **https://publisherexample.com** URL (Uniform Resource Locator), the browser connects to the respective server and renders the page on the user's device. Communication between a server and browser usually happens over the HTTPS (Hypertext Transfer Protocol Secure) encrypted protocol.

By far the most popular web browser globally is Google Chrome with approximately 64 % market share, followed by Safari (19 %), Edge (4 %), Firefox (3 %) and other smaller browsers[2]. Most of the web browsing happens on mobile devices (59 % share), followed by desktop (39 %) and tablet (2 %)[3]. Of course, these numbers vary by country – for example, Firefox has over 12 % market share in Germany[4], and Safari has 34 % share in the United States[5].

Web browsers have recently become major players in programmatic advertising, with their growing concern over user privacy. In particular, browsers have been gradually restricting the use of cookies – especially third-party, a long-time backbone of the programmatic ecosystem. Safari debuted **Intelligent Tracking Prevention (ITP)**, aimed at curbing cross-site user tracking, in 2017 and has been improving it ever since. Similarly,

Firefox launched **Enhanced Tracking Protection (ETP)** with the same aim. With its huge market share though, it's Google Chrome that really shook the market with an early 2020 announcement of upcoming third-party cookie deprecation[6].

HTML

Hypertext Markup Language (HTML) is a standard markup language used for building web pages. With the help of HTML tags, it describes web page structure so that browsers can render it correctly. For example, the **<h1> Heading example </h1>** tag indicates a heading, while **<a href="https://publisherexample.com/">Visit an awesome publisher page</a>** tag denotes a hyperlink. The tags themselves are not displayed by a browser. HTML has gone through many iterations since its inception, with the last major version being HTML5.

Beyond rendering standard web pages, HTML5 is also commonly used for building dynamic display ads which can be served programmatically. In essence, an HTML5 ad behaves like a special web page embedded within another web page. HTML5 ads range from relatively simple banners to complex rich media experiences featuring interactive elements and video. To help developers meet IAB display creative guidelines when building HTML5 ads, the Interactive Advertising Bureau publishes helpful guides[7].

HTML is designed to work in tandem with other technologies, in particular with programming languages such as JavaScript. JavaScript gives life to the web environment, enabling dynamic elements and interactions. Display ads and programmatic platform tags are often built using JavaScript.

Banner ads

A banner ad is a form of graphical advertising in digital environment, delivered by an ad server. Banner ads are an important part of the programmatic ecosystem, and having been around for a long time, are highly standardized today. The bulk of advertising inventory available programmatically can be used to serve banner ads in various forms - from simple static ads to video or interactive rich media.

Standard banner ads typically appear along the top, the bottom, or sides of a webpage in desktop environment. On mobile, popular placements for banners are along the top of the page, or further down the page embedded within content. Some common desktop formats include 300x250 pixels (Medium Rectangle), 300x600 pixels (Half-page) or 160x600 pixels (Skyscraper). On mobile, 300x250 pixels and especially responsive ads that fill various screen sizes are popular formats. The IAB (Interactive Advertising Bureau) provides detailed specifications and guidelines for the proper use of banner ads[8].

The banner ad creative is an important consideration in programmatic. In the past, banner ads for a campaign would typically comprise of one or just a handful of creatives, hard-coded into the page and served to everyone without distinction. With the advent of dynamic advertising, content of a banner ad can be generated and personalized on the fly as the webpage loads – based on data about the user who is about to see the ad, as well as other contextual information (placement, weather, events happening nearby, etc.). A typical use case for dynamic creative is product retargeting, where users are shown recently viewed products from an advertiser website within the banner ad. However, possibilities are much broader – including storytelling, or personalization for different audiences.

Common issues related to banner ads include fraud, viewability and brand safety concerns, which will be discussed in more depth later. Aggressive formats, excessive placements, and practices such as intrusive retargeting have led many users to install ad blocking software or browser plugins. Browser restrictions as well as IAB standardization helped eradicate the worst excesses, and formats are constantly evolving to be more attuned to their context and user expectations. Banner ads in particular need to adjust to new environments beyond the web browser on desktop to remain relevant. This has been successful on mobile or tablets, but less so on connected TVs.

Ad servers

An ad server is a server, used for delivery of digital ads[10]. Apart from serving ads, ad servers can fulfill several other roles, including campaign trafficking and management, optimization, metric tracking, reporting, and post-campaign analysis.

Two broad categories of ad servers exist – publisher ad servers and advertiser ad servers. For publishers, an ad server is used to manage and prioritize simultaneous campaigns from multiple clients to increase overall inventory yield. The publisher ad server has evolved to better suit programmatic world, with server-to-server SSP and DSP integrations and technologies such as header bidding. For advertisers, an ad server enables centralized campaign management across different media and publishers. Advertisers typically rely on third-party ad servers, operated by independent companies. DSPs are commonly offering integrated ad serving functionality as well.

Chapter 2
Programmatic Advertising Ecosystem

The open programmatic advertising ecosystem can be broadly divided into two distinct parts – buy side and sell side.

On the buy side, we have advertisers who purchase ad inventory for their campaigns. To do so, they usually either set up their own in-house programmatic team or employ an agency to manage programmatic buying on their behalf. Programmatic inventory buying is supported by demand-side platforms (DSPs) or custom bidders, which can participate in an open real-time bidding auction.

On the sell side are the publishers or publisher co-ops, who provide ad inventory on their properties. Publishers offer their inventory programmatically through supply-side platforms (SSPs).

Some parts of the ecosystem span both buy- and sell- sides. A key advantage of programmatic advertising is the ability to use data to increase campaign efficiency and inform inventory trading decisions. Both the sell-side as well as buy-side players can collect and take advantage of user data, which is typically facilitated through a data management platform (DMP) or a customer data platform (CDP). There are other shared components of the programmatic ecosystem as well, including various data, fraud, privacy and viewability vendors. Industry bodies and governments also play a key role in regulation, standardization and development of the ecosystem.

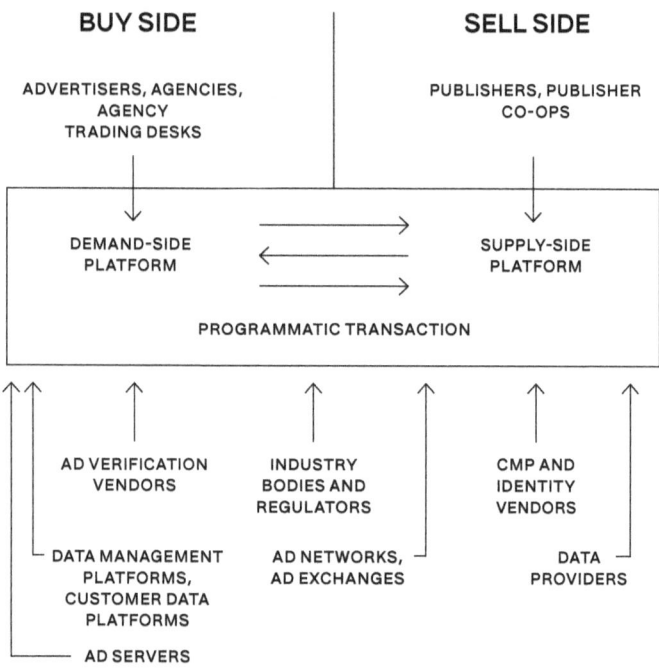

FIGURE 3: PROGRAMMATIC ADVERTISING ECOSYSTEM

Buy side

The buy side comprises of advertisers and their agencies, who purchase ad inventory programmatically using demand side platforms.

Advertisers

Advertisers are the ones fueling the rapid growth of programmatic and doing so with an increasing appetite. Their case for this trend is clear – higher advertising efficiency through automation and data. With unparalleled reach, sophisticated buying algorithms, access to premium inventory, engaging display formats and video, as well as solutions for fraud and viewability issues, programmatic is now very attractive for both performance and branding advertisers alike.

Performance advertisers were the early adopters of programmatic, since the ability to target individual users and optimize over time far outweighed initially lower inventory quality and other issues. For performance advertisers, the return on investment is key, as they tailor their campaigns towards measurable conversions. Brand advertisers are not as focused on direct impact though, but rather aim to build brand awareness and preference over time. Programmatic advertising has come a long way since the early days to become a very impactful, brand-safe environment. In addition to the open marketplace, advertisers can take advantage of private marketplaces or programmatic guaranteed.

For advertisers, the really exciting part of programmatic is the data layer behind it. They can know their customers and prospects like never before (whether directly or by using publisher first-party data), and tailor their advertising efforts on an individual level. This is a huge shift from the anonymous, affinity-based mass marketing communication of the past, with the potential that is still difficult to fully grasp. Programmatic makes efficient one-to-one marketing communication possible on an unprecedented scale, across many digital channels and formats.

Most advertisers combine retargeting with prospecting opportunities, and some have developed a significant competence in data collection and activation. More sophisticated advertisers and agencies are working on long-term data ownership, integration, analysis and enablement strategies, encompassing data from their own properties, partners or advertising campaigns. This allows advertisers and agencies to gradually improve everything from impression-level media selection and tailored creatives all the way to their actual products and services. However, with third-party cookie deprecation, advertisers will need to reinvent their data strategy to reflect this new reality.

In any case, executing a successful programmatic and data strategy requires attracting the right talent, along with suitable technology and partners. Many large advertisers have decided to move everything from programmatic media buying to data management in-house. Others work with their agencies and agency trading desks, or DSP managed services teams.

Attribution and accountability remain an issue for both performance and branding advertisers. Click-through rate (CTR) is still widely used as an efficiency metric, but mostly due to the convenience and a lack of understanding. Performance advertisers are increasingly moving towards real (and hard to manipulate) metrics such as conversions and return on investment (ROI). For brand advertisers though, metrics such as reach, frequency, or awareness/purchase intent uplift are more suitable. Moreover, they can be augmented with data and technology to account for viewability, fraud, brand safety or on-target accuracy.

Demand side platforms

A demand side platform (or DSP) is software used to purchase advertising inventory programmatically. It is the gateway to programmatic world for agencies and advertisers, who can buy advertising space centrally in an automated way on a wide range of inventory across publishers and countries. Demand side platforms serve as a focal point of programmatic campaigns, enabling design, execution, measurement, optimization and subsequent reporting of a media strategy.

DSPs are great at giving buyers a lot of control over their programmatic campaign strategies, often executed through a real-time bidding auction. Parameters such as budgets, maximum bids, timing, frequency, inventory or geography can be set according to campaign objectives. Furthermore, one can target specific audiences, and adjust bids according to the audience value to the particular advertiser. With media strategy in place, a DSP can bid with an optimal CPM for each impression in real time, considering everything it knows about the impression.

Complexity of programmatic campaigns, access to vast quantities of data, and the growing ability to process it have led to DSPs gradually becoming AI powerhouses[9]. Artificial Intelligence and machine learning are utilized to solve the biggest advertiser pain points in programmatic buying. Some of the common use cases include fraud detection, intelligent first-price auction bidding (bid shading), line item optimization, dynamic creative optimization or probabilistic cross-device solutions. For example, AI can automatically optimize hundreds of line items in real time to meet given KPIs, which would be time-consuming and less effective if performed by a human. Alternatively, AI can offer hints and recommendations to a human analyst instead of directly modifying the setup. Thanks to the rise of AI, the role of a programmatic specialist is changing from mostly executive to a combination of execution, strategy and consulting.

Many DSPs are gradually moving away from a pure play model and becoming part of broader integrated platforms. These might include for example an SSP (Supply-side platform), ad server (please note that typically clients can choose whether to serve ads directly from the DSP or use an external third-party ad server and utilize the DSP just for its bidding functionality), DMP (Data management platform), creative management, verification & measurement, or identity technologies. Such integration makes these platforms more capable and can lead to reduction of the notorious tech tax. On the other hand, lines between advertisers, publishers and technology become blurrier. For example, it is hard to optimize for highest advertiser KPIs, while also optimizing for maximum publisher yield. Good understanding of a chosen technology platform as well as transparency and trust are therefore vital.

With an ongoing industry consolidation, the number of DSP providers is gradually dwindling. Some of the notable players include The Trade Desk, Google's Display & Video 360 (or DV360, formerly DoubleClick Bid Manager), MediaMath, Xandr Invest (formerly Appnexus DSP), Amazon DSP or Adform.

Sell side

On the sell side are the publishers who provide ad inventory on their properties programmatically through supply-side platforms (SSPs).

Publishers

Publishers are key players in the open programmatic ecosystem because they control digital content (e.g. text, video or audio) and related ad inventory. They range from the premium, well-known media brands to long-tail one-person blogs. Publishers vary not only in scale, but also in the content and inventory formats they offer, as well as audiences they attract. While some publishers have been around for decades, many are products of the digital era. Programmatic advertising marks a new chapter in the ad trading history, bringing digital publishers many new challenges and opportunities.

Traditionally, big publishers sold their digital inventory through an in-house direct sales team, which negotiated inventory deals with advertisers or their agencies. With the advent of ad networks and ad exchanges, the non-premium and remnant inventory was gradually offered via non-direct channels. Programmatic advertising poses the greatest challenge to traditional direct sales models to date, as barriers to offering even the most premium inventory in an automated fashion gradually disappear. With technologies such as header bidding or server-to-server DSP to publisher ad server integrations, publishers can dynamically allocate inventory between direct and programmatic campaigns, increasing effective scale and attractiveness of biddable premium inventory.

Ultimately, with fewer sales and ad trafficking staff required, automation can bring lower costs to the publishers. On the other hand, technology and talent investment to facilitate this transition can be significant. However, even with a greater shift to programmatic, the in-house direct sales are not likely to disappear completely. Their focus will probably move to the most premium inventory, custom campaigns, and new trading models – such as programmatic guaranteed and programmatic direct in general.

Perhaps the greatest opportunity programmatic era brought to publishers is the widespread use of data to inform inventory buying decisions. Many publishers sit on valuable, large scale first-party data that can be collected, utilized and monetized. Data benefits publishers in several ways, including increased inventory value through ad targeting or user-level content customization.

As new ad formats become available for trading through programmatic channels, publishers can profit from enabling and extending their inventory. Current growth of programmatic digital video along with programmatic audio is a good example, and publishers who embrace these trends will reap the rewards.

As exciting as the programmatic era is for publishers, they are not without their share of headaches. At a breakneck pace, they must deal with many new trends and technologies which often threaten existing business models. The prime concern now is the gradual phase out of third-party cookie support in web browsers, which greatly reduces publishers' (smaller publishers' in particular) ability to outsource some of the ad tech stack necessary for monetization and to efficiently cooperate with other publishers and advertisers. Especially in Europe, publishers also need to find a way to comply with new privacy legislation such as GDPR (discussed in a separate chapter on privacy later in the book). The Transparency and Consent Framework, built by IAB Europe for this purpose, is already on its second iteration at the time of writing and is likely to undergo further changes soon. Moreover, independent publishers need to solve separate issues with mobile content monetization, adblocking, fraud, and asymmetrical competition from the closed advertising ecosystems (sometimes referred to as walled gardens). To better face these and other challenges, many publishers have chosen to cooperate in formal co-ops or more loosely on specific issues.

Supply side platforms

A supply side platform (or SSP) is software used to sell and manage advertising inventory programmatically. While DSPs are most often used by advertisers and agencies, SSPs are commonly utilized by digital publishers. SSPs are designed to maximize yield (aggregate revenue) from publisher inventory, using sophisticated rules and algorithms. Supply side platforms typically incorporate ad exchange functionality (i.e. enablement of advertising inventory transactions), which used to be distinct in the past. SSPs have the benefit of connecting publisher inventory to several demand sources – such as ad exchanges, networks and DSPs. This inventory can then be accessed by a wide range of potential buyers, who compete against each other for available impressions. A good SSP ensures that each impression has a chance to sell for the maximum price the market is willing to pay at that particular point in time – whether through a real-time auction, direct deal, or other transaction method.

Apart from connecting publishers to programmatic ecosystem, SSPs grant them a great deal of control over their inventory. Publishers can decide not only who can buy what inventory through which channels, but also what is the minimum price the inventory can be purchased for. This is accomplished by setting price floors and demand or inventory rules – options and flexibility depends on a particular SSP. For instance, a publisher might decide to completely block a particular advertiser, or only allow purchase of specific inventory if the bid is very high.

Publishers can use supply side platforms to both open up their inventory to the market in open RTB, as well as to traffic specific advertiser deals agreed by their direct sales teams. SSPs enable setup of very detailed advertiser deals, which can include variables such as price floor, inventory, formats, permitted DSPs, and even selected audience segments at which the campaign is to be targeted. Moreover, a deal can include "first look", letting the advertiser purchase impressions falling within the deal before anyone else. This so-called preferred deal usually carries a premium price though.

Just like many DSPs, some SSPs are gradually expanding their offering to include bidding functionality and other technologies. The line between SSPs, DSPs, DMPs and other ad tech vendor types is becoming blurrier. Some of the well-known supply side platforms are Magnite (formerly Rubicon Project), Xandr Monetize (formerly AppNexus), PubMatic, Index Exchange or Google's Ad Manager.

Other ecosystem participants

Some parts of the ecosystem span both buy- and sell- sides. A key advantage of programmatic advertising is the ability to use data to increase campaign efficiency and inform inventory trading decisions. Both the sell-side as well as buy-side players can collect and take advantage of user data, which is typically facilitated through a data management platform (DMP) or a customer data platform (CDP). Data, particularly for audience targeting, can also be purchased from specialized vendors. Data-related ecosystem participants will be covered in a separate chapter dedicated to advertising data.

There are other shared components of the programmatic ecosystem as well, including ad servers as well as identity, fraud, privacy and viewability vendors. Industry bodies and governments also play a key role in regulation, standardization and development of the ecosystem.

Ad verification vendors

Specialized brand safety, fraud prevention and viewability measurement (jointly referred to as ad verification) vendors are now an integral part of the programmatic ecosystem. They ensure ad inventory supply quality primarily on behalf of advertisers, helping to drive overall ecosystem trust and transparency. Some of the key vendors include Moat, DoubleVerify or Integral Ad Science.

Consent management platform vendors

Ever since the General Data Protection Regulation (GDPR) came into effect, to be later joined by the California Consumer Privacy Act (CCPA), it is necessary to ask users for their consent with data collection and processing (more detail in a separate chapter on privacy later in this book). Consent Management Platforms (CMPs) are generally used for this purpose in the open digital advertising ecosystem, and many vendors have sprung up to support both publishers and advertisers. Some of the popular options include OneTrust, Didomi, Cookiebot, Quantcast or TrustArc.

Identity providers and initiatives

With the gradual deprecation of third-party cookies in web browsers, it is increasingly difficult to maintain stable user identity for the purpose of ad targeting, optimization or campaign measurement. This is discussed more in a separate chapter on identity. At this point though, it is important to note that several identity vendors and initiatives are currently attempting to address this issue. These include for example Unified ID 2.0, ID5, European netID or Czech Ad ID.

Ad servers

Ad servers are used by advertisers and publishers to deliver digital ads. They not only serve ads, but also help with campaign trafficking, management, optimization, tracking, reporting and analysis. Advertisers use ad servers (typically integrated with their DSPs of choice) to centralize campaign management across different media and publishers. On the other side, publishers use them to manage and prioritize simultaneous direct and programmatic campaigns. To do so, publishers integrate their ad servers with selected SSPs using either a direct server-to-server communication, or via header bidding. Some of the well-known ad servers include Google Ad Manager, Sizmek, Equativ (formerly Smart) or Adform.

Industry bodies

Programmatic advertising is by now a fairly mature industry, with several bodies contributing to its development and regulation. Perhaps the most prominent is the Interactive Advertising Bureau, along with local and regional regulators who are playing an increasingly important role.

Interactive Advertising Bureau

The Interactive Advertising Bureau (IAB)[11] is a trade organization with over 700 members, including media and technology companies in the digital advertising space. The IAB is particularly influential in the United States (where it represents around 86 percent of online advertising) and Europe. It was founded in 1996 and is headquartered in New York city.

Interactive Advertising Bureau leads the industry in many areas and is key for programmatic advertising growth. It facilitates development of important standards, such as OpenRTB, OpenDirect or Transparency and Consent Framework in Europe, enabling programmatic ad trading among many diverse market players. The IAB also conducts research, and publishes white papers, guidelines and best practices on a wide range of industry topics. Member education is key, and the IAB offers a range of webinars, classes, training programs and even a professional certification. There is a plethora of events organized or supported by the IAB, from council and committee meetings to major industry conferences.

The IAB is also very active when it comes to public policy, where it represents the interests of its members and the digital industry. It strives to promote self-regulation, and shape legislation in a way that enables digital advertising growth and development.

Trustworthy Accountability Group

The Trustworthy Accountability Group[12] (TAG) is a joint project created by the IAB, American Association of Advertising Agencies (4A's) and Association of National Advertisers (ANA). TAG aims to increase transparency and accountability across the digital ad industry, focusing on eliminating fraudulent traffic, combating malware, combating ad-supported internet piracy and promoting brand safety.

Media Rating Council

The Media Rating Council's[14] objective is to secure valid, reliable and effective audience measurement services for the media industry and related users. It also aims to evolve and determine minimum disclosure and ethical criteria for media audience measurement services, and to provide and administer an audit system designed to inform users as to whether such audience measurements are conducted in conformance with the criteria and procedures developed. The Council seeks to improve quality of audience measurement by rating services and to provide a better understanding of the applications and limitations of rating information. For example, the MRC is responsible for setting the display advertising viewability standards used within the programmatic ecosystem.

Other industry bodies and regulators

There are of course other industry organizations contributing to development, standardization and self-regulation of programmatic advertising. These include for example the American Association of Advertising Agencies (4A's) and Association of National Advertisers (ANA), as well as the Digital Advertising Alliance (DAA) or Direct Marketing Association (DMA). Naturally, similar bodies exist in many countries across the globe.

Government influence and regulation plays a key role as well. The Federal Trade Commission (FTC) is particularly important in the US, while the European Commission strives to regulate the European market. National laws further regulate programmatic and other forms of advertising on a country level.

Chapter 3
Programmatic Standards

Now that we introduced programmatic ecosystem players, let's look at how they interact and which tools and strategies they use to succeed in programmatic advertising. In this chapter, we will start by outlining the basic programmatic transaction types. We will explore both auction-based, as well as fixed price transactions, and the underlying protocols and standards that enable them. In the second part of this chapter, we will follow up with some practical considerations and techniques commonly used in programmatic trading.

Programmatic transaction types

Programmatic advertising currently encompasses four basic transaction types – open auction, PMP auction (which stands for private marketplace, also known as invitation-only auction), preferred deal (also known as unreserved fixed rate) and programmatic guaranteed[15].

These transaction types are differentiated by two main factors – whether an auction is involved in determining inventory price, and whether the inventory is reserved or not. A common misconception equates auction-based transaction types (commonly referred to as RTB, or real-time bidding) with programmatic advertising, ignoring fixed-price transaction types.

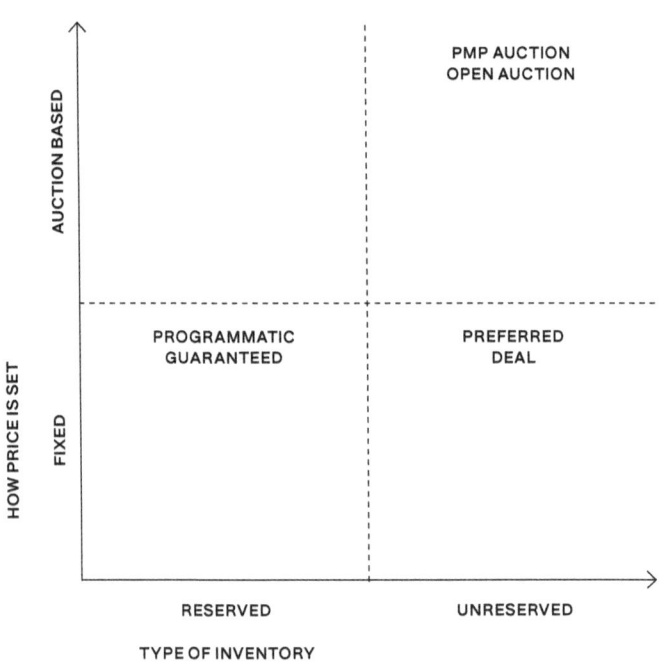

FIGURE 4: PROGRAMMATIC TRANSACTION TYPES

Auction-based transaction types

If an auction is involved in setting inventory price, we talk about either open auction, or PMP auction. In both cases, inventory is unreserved, and real-time bidding technology underlies ad inventory buying.

OPEN AUCTION

Open auction (also known as open marketplace or open exchange) is a very common programmatic transaction type and is generally accessible to all buyers. It tends to have low priority in publisher monetization setups, behind PMP auction, preferred deals or direct deals (whether legacy insertion orders or programmatic guaranteed). Publishers set floor prices for their inventory to both protect other deal types as well as maintain inventory value. Publishers can also restrict access to some buyers via blocklists or individual inventory price floors. To further protect direct sales and other more premium channels, publishers sometimes mask URLs in an open auction (multiple domains are grouped under the same URL), or the auction is completely blind (URL is not disclosed at all).

PMP AUCTION

Unlike an open auction, PMP auction (private marketplace, or officially invitation-only auction) is exclusive to a limited number of advertisers selected by the publisher.

PMP advertisers get better access to publisher inventory (with higher priority compared to open auction), while the publisher can command higher CPM. To make this auction format even more attractive, publishers can for instance offer transparent URLs, access to more premium inventory, or exclusive first-party data.

Private marketplace is considered one of the programmatic direct transaction types alongside preferred deals and programmatic guaranteed. Programmatic direct transaction types involve pre-negotiation of terms between the publisher and selected advertisers, encapsulated in a deal with a corresponding deal ID.

The Deal ID is a unique identifier designed to help buyers and sellers set up custom programmatic deals. When advertisers and publishers negotiate a deal (regardless of the actual transaction type), they can for instance agree a certain price floor (or fixed price), inventory, targeting, priority, or URL transparency. When a deal is set up in the SSP, a unique Deal ID is generated to identify it. The Deal ID becomes another attribute of the bid request, signifying that all bid requests containing this Deal ID are only for impressions with agreed parameters. This way, DSPs and SSPs know that a particular bid request or response is related to a specific deal and behave accordingly.

CHAPTER 3   PROGRAMMATIC STANDARDS

Fixed price transaction types

With fixed price transaction types, there's no auction involved in setting inventory price. Two common fixed price deal types exist - preferred deals and programmatic guaranteed.

PREFERRED DEAL

In a preferred deal (officially called unreserved fixed rate), the advertiser and publisher agree on a fixed price and first-look access to inventory. The advertiser has an option to bid on eligible and interesting impressions but is not obligated to do so. A preferred deal guarantees visibility of the entire inventory to the advertiser thanks to first-look priority, and is a more premium transaction type than standard PMP or open auction. Preferred deals sometimes get grouped under PMP though in practice.

PROGRAMMATIC GUARANTEED

With programmatic guaranteed, also known as automated direct or programmatic premium, the price is fixed, and the inventory is guaranteed. Automated guaranteed is like traditional direct sales, but with the advantage of automation. Such deals are typically negotiated and agreed by publishers' sales teams and trafficked programmatically alongside other transaction types. With automated guaranteed, unlike auction-based transaction types, advertisers typically cannot pick individual impressions they might be more interested in.

Automating the direct sales process can mean significant time savings on both buy and sell sides. With simpler workflow, fewer ad operations staff are needed to traffic and manage digital campaigns. There's also a lower risk of human error, or unnecessary set up delays. Compared to auction-based transaction types, automated guaranteed offers advertisers an assurance that their campaign will achieve required impression volume. Other benefits, such as the option to use data for targeting, are shared with other programmatic transaction types.

Trading standards

To simplify communication between buyers and suppliers of inventory in the programmatic ecosystem, protocol standards have been developed to support all basic transaction types. OpenRTB[16], originally started in 2010 as a pilot project between a handful of DSPs and SSPs, has now been adopted as an IAB standard. The OpenRTB protocol is maintained and continuously improved by the RTB Project, a working group within IAB Technology Council. Existing separately alongside OpenRTB, OpenDirect is a standard for buying and selling automated guaranteed ad inventory. The aim of these protocols is not only to simplify communication, but also to enable greater innovation and growth within programmatic.

There are other standards helping the ecosystem run smoothly and solving specific challenges as they emerge. These include for example Ads.txt, Sellers.json, VAST, Open Measurement SDK or Transparency and Consent Framework (TCF is covered separately in a chapter on privacy).

OpenRTB

As noted in the latest OpenRTB protocol version (2.6 at the time of writing[17]), the overall goal of OpenRTB is to create a lingua franca for communicating between buyers and sellers. It aims to make integration between parties easier, so that innovation can happen at a deeper-level at each of the businesses in the ecosystem. In the following section, we will briefly look at both the protocol and basic auction flow.

OPENRTB PROTOCOL

OpenRTB API specification is a very detailed guide to the real-time bidding interface. It describes basic interactions taking place between an exchange and bidders, including bid requests, bid responses, win notices and ad markups. Each interaction must follow a prescribed format and contain a number of attributes – some of which are required, and others recommended or optional. For example, a bid request must contain information such as unique auction ID, one or several impression IDs, and impression type (banner, video or native) for each impression offered. Other attributes of the bid request can include site (or app), device and user information, or the minimum bid.

In addition to describing the content and the structure of basic RTB interactions, OpenRTB protocol suggests JSON as the ideal data format. As for video, OpenRTB protocol assumes compliance with VAST standard. Additional, more granular specifications also fall under this standard, such as Native Ad Specification or support for audio ad units. While fairly prescriptive, OpenRTB protocol still leaves room for customization – for instance, exchanges can offer additional data formats, or exchange-specific extensions to the standard. The full specification can be downloaded from IAB website[18].

OPENRTB AUCTION FLOW

Given that auction-based transaction types currently make up the bulk of programmatic advertising, it is very useful to understand how a real-time bidding auction works.

An auction enables buying and selling of individual ad impressions in a fraction of a second, letting all participants trade each impression at its current market price. Every real-time bidding auction follows a process established by the OpenRTB protocol. An auction happens in real time (while the user is waiting for a page to load), and typically takes less than 100 milliseconds. A separate auction is usually held for each available impression on the page. The auction proceeds in the following eight steps:

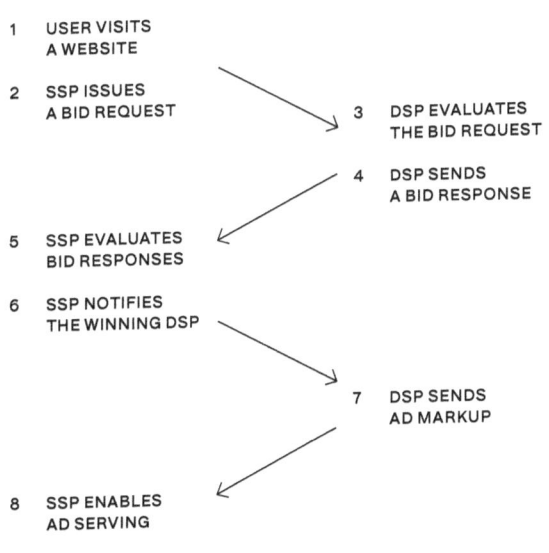

FIGURE 5: OPEN RTB AUCTION FLOW

1) User visits a website

When a user visits a publisher website, their browser requests content from various sources in order to render the page. Some of the content will come directly from publisher servers (usually main content, such as an article or a video the user came to see). Ads, however, might come from elsewhere, particularly with an RTB auction. In a real-time bidding auction, the request to fill an available ad slot typically goes from a publisher page to a publisher ad server, which (under pre-defined conditions) redirects the request to a Supply-side platform.

2) Supply-side platform issues a bid request

SSP handles the auction for an available impression on behalf of a publisher. It issues a bid request to all Demand-side platforms which might participate in the auction. The bid request contains information which can be useful to the participating parties in making an informed decision about a bid. As noted previously, OpenRTB protocol defines which parameters are required, recommended or optional in a bid request. A bid request can also contain data related to the user who is about to see an ad, making the impression potentially more valuable to some advertisers.

3) Demand-side platform evaluates the bid request

Upon receiving the bid request, a DSP will determine how valuable the impression is, and whether to participate in the auction. Several factors can play a role – such as publisher, placement, floor price, user id, user value or constraints like frequency caps or budget limits.

4) Demand-side platform sends a bid response
If a DSP decides to participate in the auction (i.e. the bid request falls within the rules set up in the DSP for a particular campaign), it will issue a bid response. Just like a bid request, the bid response has a specific format outlined in the OpenRTB protocol. A bid response contains one or several bids from various seats (i.e. buyers, usually different advertisers or agencies) under the same DSP, or even from the same seat (one advertiser/agency with several campaigns). A bid response usually includes Ad Markup (Ad Tag or Ad serving code, so the ad can be rendered).

5) Supply-side platform evaluates bid responses
The SSP gathers all bid responses from participating DSPs and picks a winner under the auction rules. The impression is usually awarded to the highest bidder (at a price submitted in the bid, in a so-called first-price auction). However, other criteria might come into play – some advertisers could be blocked by the publisher for instance, so they cannot win the auction.

6) Supply-side platform notifies the winning DSP
The SSP sends a win notice to the winning DSP, which includes the settlement price. Loss notice is not issued in real time to other participants (but lost bid data can be shared later in a separate process).

7) Demand-side platform sends Ad Markup
In case the DSP didn't already send Ad Markup in a bid response, it must be sent at this point. Ad Markup is normally sent in a bid response though.

8) Supply-side platform enables ad serving
Concluding the real-time bidding auction, SSP passes Ad Markup of the winning bidder along to a user's browser. Ad is then served, together with other content on the web page. All these steps happen so fast that users can't even notice an auction happening in the background, while a page is loading.

OpenDirect

OpenDirect API specification supports the execution of automated guaranteed campaigns. In programmatic guaranteed, the deal is negotiated directly between buyer and seller (in-person or via a platform), the inventory and pricing are guaranteed, and the campaign runs at the same priority as other direct deals in the ad server.

The RFP (Request for Proposal) and campaign trafficking process are completely automated within the technology platform[19].

Other standards

Naturally, there is a vast array of ever evolving standards to capture the complexity of programmatic advertising ecosystem. An overview of the most important ones can be found on IAB Tech Lab website[20].
For example, Ads.txt is an IAB Tech Lab standard which specifies a mechanism for publishers to list their authorized digital sellers, to fight against fraud and misrepresented domains[21]. Sellers.json provides a mechanism to enable buyers to discover who the entities are that are either direct sellers of (provided they are ads.txt authorized) or intermediaries in the selling of digital advertising[22]. Programmatic video ads have their own set of standards to facilitate trading among multiple parties. A prominent standard is Video Ad Serving Template (VAST), used for structuring ad tags that video and audio ads to media players. Using an XML schema, VAST transfers important metadata about an ad from the ad server to a media player[23]. The Open Measurement Software Development Kit (OM SDK) is designed to facilitate third party viewability and verification measurement for ads served to web video and mobile app environments[24].

First-price auction

Although not a standard in a strict sense, it is important to understand that real-time bidding auctions in the open ecosystem generally follow a first-price auction model. In a first-price auction model, bidders pay exactly what they bid[25]. This is a departure from second-price auction model that was characteristic for RTB just a few years ago. In second-price auction, a winning bidder pays the second-highest bid amount plus $0.01.

The shift from second-price auction to first-price auction brought with it more transparency and enabled an efficient unified auction with multiple bidders alongside direct campaigns on the publisher side (implemented either using header bidding or server-to-server ad server integrations).

Chapter 4
Trading in Practice

Having introduced programmatic transaction types and the standards that govern their execution, let us briefly discuss some of the tools, considerations and challenges in the practice of trading. This is not exhaustive by any means, but rather a selection of concepts that are useful to understand when starting out in programmatic. We will first go over the buy side, then look at the sell side, and finally consider issues that span both transaction sides.

Buy side

On the buy side, we will cover buying algorithms, bid shading, frequency capping, measurement and attribution as well as supply-path optimization. All these topics are complex and worth diving into in more detail beyond this book.

Buying algorithms

Programmatic buying execution via demand-side platforms is quickly evolving from a largely manual affair to an increasingly automated process. DSPs are investing into machine learning applications to bring new campaign management tools that are more efficient than humans. One category of these tools comprises of buying algorithms, which range from basic buying enablers to sophisticated outcome-based trading engines.

Perhaps the most basic buying algorithm is **Fixed CPM**. The DSP simply bids with a specified CPM, which is equal to the final purchase price if the bid wins an auction. While simple to understand and use, a buyer risks paying more for some impressions that could have been purchased with a lower bid. This buying algorithm is often used with publisher deals, where price is agreed beforehand.

More sophisticated variants of CPM-based algorithms include **Viewable CPM** or **Dynamic CPM**. With Viewable CPM, a DSP optimizes its bidding to achieve a specified CPM for viewable impressions. To define which impressions count as viewable, either Media Rating Council/Interactive Advertising Bureau or custom advertiser standard can be used. Dynamic CPM automatically lowers bids whenever possible below a specified maximum to achieve the lowest possible cost while maintaining campaign win rate and pacing. This is called bid shading and is explained later in this chapter.

Other commonly used buying algorithms focus on cost per desired outcome. **Cost per click** algorithm optimizes towards a desired cost per click on an ad. **Cost per acquisition (CPA)** aims to achieve a specified conversion cost. **Return on advertising spend (ROAS)** algorithm tries to maintain a set return on investment while bidding, considering the value of resulting conversions.

Bid shading

Recent shift to first-price auction in real-time bidding brought with it a new challenge to advertisers. They need to optimize their bids and avoid overpaying for impressions, as they can no longer rely on the market to establish impression value through second-price auction. To help the advertisers, DSPs (albeit initially even some SSPs) have developed a technique called bid shading. Bid shading is an algorithm that uses historical bids and win rate to calculate an optimal bid for a given impression. In effect, bid shading lowers average bid below what an advertiser might be willing to pay as a maximum bid, saving costs while maintaining a satisfactory win rate.

Frequency capping

Another area where DSPs add a lot of value to advertisers is campaign frequency capping. Advertisers can typically set the maximum number of impressions per user (usually per day, campaign or a more sophisticated combination). This increases campaign efficiency with less wasted impressions on user overexposure, while at the same time offering users a better advertising experience. With third-party cookies, a user was typically approximated as a unique cookie ID (so a single real person would have multiple IDs, for each browser on every device they used). This worked well enough but is no longer viable with first-party cookie IDs which are unique per domain (so each user can easily have tens or hundreds of IDs). Frequency capping without third-party cookies is a real challenge for DSPs, and solutions are emerging to address this. Campaigns can for example be restricted to a single domain, which is possible with large publishers. Or an ID solution (probabilistic or deterministic) can help stitch user identities across domains and devices. It remains to be seen how frequency capping evolves to meet the expectations of users and advertisers as technology landscape evolves.

Measurement

Next, let us briefly discuss campaign measurement options offered by DSPs. As a standard, demand-side platforms provide measurement of impressions, clicks and conversions. However, they differ in the sophistication of their measurement tools, variety of metrics, and trust in the reported numbers. For example, a DSP might be able to measure impression viewability, time in view, or user engagement. When it comes to conversions, DSPs need to model those that cannot be directly measured or attributed to a campaign (typically due to lack of identity or user consent, as discussed later in this book). It is a common practice for demand-side platforms to directly integrate third-party measurement vendors to give their clients more flexibility. The ability of a DSP to measure campaign performance is directly tied to its ability to use the resulting data for attribution and campaign optimization. In other words, measurement is vital to delivering efficiency and ROI to clients, and to being able to prove it. It remains to be seen how the ongoing changes to identity and privacy landscape play out in this regard.

Attribution

Very closely related to measurement is the topic of attribution. It is helpful to view attribution as a tool for optimizing marketing spend to maximize return on investment. In an ideal world, marketers would know exactly how each part of their communication mix contributed to a desired outcome (usually conversions), and attribute credit accordingly. Activities which deliver the highest incremental return on investment would then receive a bigger portion of the marketing budget, while those that don't contribute would be cut from the plan. Eventually, budget should be allocated in an optimal way for maximum ROI. In reality, attribution is not nearly this straightforward, and can be tricky (if not impossible) to implement in a true and useful way.

Some of the reasons for the difficulty of proper attribution (even within a digital ecosystem, not considering offline world) include measurement restrictions, identity resolution limitations and selection of an attribution algorithm. First, many closed advertising ecosystems restrict third-party measurement. Without it, it is not possible to track user journeys across multiple channels from a single point as a foundation for attributing a conversion. Second, even if measurement was not restricted, the user identity landscape is very fragmented and further crumbling. This makes it almost impossible to reliably reconstruct deduplicated user journeys. Third, selecting the right algorithm for maximum ROI is not an easy task even with all the required data.

The fate of cross-channel attribution is unclear at the moment, although given the changes to identity and privacy it seems like a dream of the past. Advertisers might need to rely on (often opaque) attribution models built into siloed advertising ecosystems and find new ways to optimize overall advertising spend.

Supply-path optimization

Supply-path optimization (SPO) is a process of finding the optimal way for buyers to purchase advertising inventory. SPO is both a genuine effort as well as marketing buzzword, and there isn't a clear industry consensus on its definition or merit. For certain buyers though, primarily large media agencies and tier one advertisers, the benefits are clear and worthwhile.

SPO emerged as a reaction to publishers widely adopting header bidding. With the rise of header bidding, whereby multiple SSPs can compete for the same impression simultaneously, the number of paths towards that impression has exploded. Things used to be much simpler with legacy waterfall setups on the publisher side - the order of preference for monetization, and in turn impression access, was given. Header bidding evened out the playing field, but at the same time incentivized publishers to integrate many additional supply partners. While mostly beneficial to publishers, this has some negative consequences on the buy side.

Having too many SSPs competing simultaneously for the same impression in a header bidding auction can lead to some buyer headaches. These include overwhelming of a buyer's demand-side platform, risk of fraud, low auction transparency and cost inefficiencies. DSPs must handle an order of magnitude more bid requests than before (also referred to as bid duplication), and due to increased complexity risk bidding against themselves. Some long-tail supply partners might be more prone to fraud given the necessary investment to combat it. Auction transparency decreases and fees become muddled, with impressions being passed around many technology partners before being finally sold. Finally, large advertisers and agencies cannot effectively exercise economies of scale to lower their technology fees.

Some of the main potential advantages of SPO include better buyer fees, more data & transparency, and more influence over technology partners and their development roadmaps. Generally, these are benefits of consolidation, and can give advantage to those players who have the expertise and budget size to do it effectively. With the right supply partners, larger advertisers can find themselves in more control of their investment and long-term strategy.

While the idea of SPO and its potential benefits are clear, it is not always straightforward to execute on it. Overall, SPO is both a manual as well as increasingly automated process. Negotiating with and analyzing supply partners, coordinating with buyers' DSPs and using some of the SPO tools (e.g. turning off selected SSPs) relies on highly skilled programmatic professionals. At the same time, DSPs are introducing automated SPO tools built on machine learning. These analyze and optimize buying paths in real time in accordance with buyer or agency SPO strategy. At the same time, automated SPO shields a DSP from having to process excessive number of bid requests. However, it is important that DSPs also provide buyers manual SPO controls to override any algorithmic SPO decisioning so that their media buying behaviors across trading teams and business lines are enforced and followed for strategic alignment top to bottom[26].

As supply-path optimization quickly becomes an established process, focus has now broadened to sell-side with the advent of demand-path optimization (DPO). Mirroring SPO, DPO is a process of finding the optimal way for sellers to sell advertising inventory. For example, an SSP with better audience match rates makes it the optimal route for retargeting campaigns, for example, while campaigns that deal with high-value inventory, such as direct deals, CTV and video, are better off going through an SSP with a lower take rate fee[27].

SPO is without a doubt an important and welcome trend. Lowering of the programmatic tech tax, closer cooperation, consolidation which enables innovation, and more transparency are certainly good for the ecosystem. On the other hand, there is a risk of decreased industry competition and even more market power in the hands of a few bigger players. In any case, SPO is a sign of programmatic advertising reaching a more mature stage, with all its pros and cons.

Sell side

On the publisher side, perhaps the most important thing for programmatic buyers to understand is the yield management setup of their supply partners. This governs their ability to access inventory and the price it can be purchased at. Conversely, a major task for publishers is to manage their inventory in a way that maximizes yield while ensuring quality of their demand partners. In this section, we will cover yield management setup options, including waterfall, header bidding and direct server-to-server integrations.

Yield management setup

Yield management is an optimization technique used by publishers to maximize ad revenue from available impressions in a constantly shifting demand landscape. Larger publishers employ whole yield management teams for this task and have many options when it comes to monetizing their inventory in the open programmatic ecosystem. They can opt for a pure programmatic model, or a combination with other sources of demand such as direct campaigns (i.e. insertion orders). Two common yield management approaches for more complex setups are waterfall and a unified auction.

With a waterfall setup, publishers usually fill available impressions through demand from various sources in a decreasing order of priority. Direct campaigns typically have the highest priority, whether programmatic or not. If an impression is not filled by a direct campaign, it is usually offered in a private and subsequently open auction.

Each publisher can have a different default priority order, with lots of options for individual tweaks on a deal/campaign basis. Deals can for instance include first-look, giving a selected advertiser the option to purchase impressions ahead of anyone else. However complex though, waterfall setups are created manually based on historical data and business considerations. This leads to sub-optimal overall yield for publishers, and restricted inventory access for advertisers. Many publishers have therefore replaced legacy waterfall setup with unified auction.

With a unified auction, demand sources can compete for impressions on a more level playing field, using price as a primary deciding factor. A unified auction is usually achieved with the help of header bidding, server-to-server integrations or a combination of the two. Unified auction has the advantage of increased competition for each individual impression and in turn higher yield for publishers. Publishers still retain control over auction participants, and their prioritization beyond the highest bid. For example, a publisher can still choose to award an impression to a participant who didn't submit the highest bid, if other considerations (such as a contractual agreement) warrant this. Advertisers benefit from a unified auction as well, as they gain potential access to the entire publisher inventory.

HEADER BIDDING

In essence, header bidding technology enables a publisher to solicit bids for each impression from multiple demand sources simultaneously, rather than sequentially (as in waterfall setup). This gives every demand source potentially equal inventory access, and the increased competition for each impression translates into higher effective CPM and overall publisher revenue.

Exact implementation of header bidding will vary by publisher and specific circumstances, but the technology is usually based on a JavaScript tag placed in the header section of a website (hence the name). This piece of code initiates a preliminary auction, inviting integrated partners to submit actual bids for the offered inventory. Alternatively, publishers can implement server-side header bidding where auction happens on a server rather than a browser. Armed with real-time impression value information, a publisher ad server can then dynamically prioritize demand sources (such as directly sold campaigns, demand from SSPs, or retargeters) to maximize yield.

Header bidding is not entirely without issues. Since a JavaScript tag is implemented in the website header, some publishers might be worried about slow page loading. Header bidding is typically implemented asynchronously though, to avoid page latency. Another issue is a limit on the number of demand sources publishers choose to integrate into the header auction. Other demand sources can participate indirectly through one of the integrated ones, but typically need to pay transaction fees which puts them at a disadvantage[28]. This can lead to market consolidation and decreased competition. Also, compared to direct server-to-server integrations, bid granularity in the publisher ad server can be lower with header bidding leading to some inefficiency.

SERVER-TO-SERVER INTEGRATIONS

Direct server-to-server integrations between publisher ad server and selected SSPs enable a more efficient unified auction. Please note this is a different concept than client or server-side header bidding. With a direct integration, an SSP can bypass header auction altogether. This has the benefit of being able to pass exact bids to the ad server (with header bidding, bids can be translated into bands in the process with less granularity) and closer relationship with the publisher. The exact setup will vary by publisher, but often there would be a combination of some SSPs with a server-to-server integrations to the ad server and some integrated via header bidding.

Programmatic trading issues

In the final section of this chapter, we will discuss three common issues that impact programmatic trading on both the advertiser as well as publisher sides. These include fraud, viewability and ad blocking.

Fraud

In the digital advertising world, fraud is a broad term encompassing a wide range of unethical (or outright illegal) activities, designed to stealthily divert some of the advertising spend into the pockets of its perpetrators. Fraudsters attempt to game the advertising ecosystem by artificially inflating metrics such as impressions, clicks or conversions, while masquerading as organic activity. They appear to create value for advertisers, but in fact deliver no real impact.

Probably the most common type of fraud is nonhuman traffic (NHT), where deceptive computer programs (bots) mimic desired behavior of real users on the web. Bots are used to register impressions, clicks or influence other metrics, pretending they are actual humans. More sophisticated bots can fake conversions (for example fill out a lead-generation form) or let themselves be retargeted. This type of fraud is so prevalent, that the term "fraud" is often used interchangeably with NHT. Exact scale of nonhuman traffic is not known, as it varies greatly by region, publisher, or exchange.

There are other types of fraud besides nonhuman traffic. Ads can be for example served stacked on top of each other, or in tiny 1x1 pixel frames. Publisher domain might also be manipulated to make inventory appear more valuable – so called domain laundering. Fraudsters also set up networks of fake sites, built only for advertising with no valuable content (and usually with very little human traffic).

As part of an industry-wide effort to tackle fraud, IAB formed the Trustworthy Accountability Group (TAG)[29], which was already introduced in chapter two. Also, new tools such as ads.txt, app-ads.txt[30] or sellers.json[31] have emerged to help eradicate fraud. While TAG and other organizations offer insights and direction on how to tackle fraud, responsibility for eradicating it lies with every honest participant in the digital advertising ecosystem – particularly publishers and advertisers.

Publishers differ in their stance towards fraud. To most legitimate and premium publishers, fraud is a serious issue as it devalues honest impressions seen by real humans. If fraud was eradicated, these publishers would profit substantially. On the other hand, there are publishers who thrive on fraud. Their business models are often based on arbitrage – buying cheap, mostly nonhuman traffic, and turning it into more expensive impressions sold to advertisers. Such arbitrage models would not work with real human traffic, as it is too expensive to purchase.

Advertisers stand to lose the most to ad fraud, as their budgets could be diverted from campaigns and deliver no impact in return. One way to combat ad fraud is to look beyond simple metrics when analyzing campaigns (impressions or CTR for example), as these are easy to manipulate artificially. Instead, advertisers should focus more on the end goal metrics, such as return on investment or real conversions. As fraudulent activities have net negative ROI, advertisers who optimize towards the right metrics should be able to eliminate most of them from their campaigns. Of course, it is hard to use such metrics for evaluating branding campaigns. Here, advertisers can get help from a number of vendors specializing in ad fraud identification and filtering (often alongside viewability measurement). Some of the well-known players offering anti-fraud solutions include DoubleVerify or Integral Ad Science.

Fraud is often discussed together with viewability, albeit they are fundamentally different issues. With fraud, the question is typically whether an ad was served to a human. Viewability then determines if that human had an opportunity to see the ad. However, both issues are related to advertising efficiency. If advertisers spend part of their budgets on ads which are served to bots, or which could never have been seen by human users, their return-on-investment decreases. It must be noted though, that solving ad fraud comes before solving viewability – if an impression gets served to a bot, it doesn't matter anymore whether it was viewable or not.

Viewability

Ad viewability is broadly defined as the opportunity for an ad to be seen. It has become an important issue, as many advertisers realized that a large proportion of impressions they pay for not only goes unseen, but could never have been seen by human users in the first place. This is due to several reasons, some more legitimate than others. For example, users might scroll through a page too quickly to have a chance to see an ad. Or the ads might be served on a page section that never comes into view of the user (below the fold for example). Many impressions are also served fraudulently, especially to non-human traffic.

The Media Rating Council (MRC) classifies an ad impression as viewable, if at least 50 % of the ad pixels were contained in the viewable space of the browser window, on an in-focus browser tab, for at least one continuous second post ad render. For larger formats, 30 % of the ad pixels are sufficient to qualify within this definition. Video ad impressions require 50 % of the pixels for two seconds to be considered viewable. Requirements are the same for mobile viewability (50 % of pixels for one second for display, two seconds for video), both on mobile web and within apps.

Ad viewability rates vary across publishers, (usually in the range of 50-70 %), depending on inventory quality and viewability measurement vendor. Although some advertisers would like to see 100 % viewability for their campaigns, the currently accepted standard is 70 % (but is entirely up to the parties involved), due to technological and commercial limitations. IAB considers the 70 % standard only temporary, with a view of increasing it in the future.

Major vendors are accredited by the MRC, and many offer measurement options beyond the minimum viewability standard. Some of the well-known players in this space include DoubleVerify, Integral Ad Science or Moat.

Viewability is a hot topic not only for advertisers, but also for publishers. They need to know what the viewability rate of their inventory is with different providers, to guarantee viewability thresholds to advertisers. Given the differences in reported viewability among vendors, publishers are in a difficult situation. If an advertiser is using a different viewability vendor than a publisher, there is a high chance of discrepancy and potential under-delivery. It might be safer to over-deliver, but this represents inefficiency on the publisher side. Inventory forecasting in this situation can become a nightmare.

With all the buzz surrounding viewability, it is good to keep in mind that a viewable ad was not necessarily seen, let alone engaged with. Viewability by itself doesn't guarantee impact, and too much emphasis on this single metric might even be counterproductive. To illustrate, one way to increase campaign viewability rate is to use smaller ad formats, which tend to have a higher chance of meeting the MRC viewability standard compared to large formats. Smaller formats, albeit viewable, are often ignored by users though – generating no impact at all. Viewability therefore needs to be considered in the context of engagement and results, not just as a stand-alone metric.

Ad blocking

Ad blocking is a very common practice of using a program to remove advertising while browsing the internet or using apps. Although exact numbers vary, it is clear that ad blocking is prevalent among younger demographics (particularly young males), and in some regions – including Germany and central/eastern Europe.

Reasons for ad blocking popularity are straightforward. Many users find that there are too many low quality or annoying ads on their favorite websites, and are tired of always having to look for the elusive x to close an ad. The widespread practice of retargeting is partly to blame as well, increasing privacy concerns. Ads (particularly rich media and some novel formats) can have negative impact on page load times – this is even worse on mobile, where the connection speed and data plans are still a significant limitation.

Ad blocking is a major problem for many publishers and app developers, who depend on advertising as their main source of revenue. For years, there used to be a clear (albeit often not understood) value exchange between publishers and consumers – free content for exposure to advertising. Ad blocking breaks this value exchange, as publishers no longer get anything back for the content that often costs a lot to produce. Some of the value just disappears, while ad blocking companies try to capture the rest by having publishers and advertisers pay for whitelisting their ads. This practice is highly controversial and subject to legal disputes. The strongest weapon publishers have in fighting ad blocking is provision of genuine value, high standard of advertising and careful communication with their users.

Chapter 5
Data

Data is the lifeblood of programmatic advertising. While automation makes ad buying process more efficient, it is data that elevates programmatic to its game-changer status. Publishers, and to some extent ad tech platforms and advertisers, can know internet users like never before, and use this information within the programmatic ecosystem to individually tailor communication on an unprecedented scale. Data also enables automation to deliver desired campaign KPIs, with extreme efficiency. This is a true marketing revolution, and data is front and center.

Data in digital advertising is an incredibly complex topic, and this chapter only gives a broad introduction. Readers who would like to know a bit more will find an in-depth exploration in a complementary book, "Data in Digital Advertising." In this chapter, we will cover some basics related to advertising data - including an overview of sources, data creation methods, and common categorizations. Then we'll briefly discuss the data ecosystem, before closing the chapter with a look at some data activation strategies such as prospecting or retargeting.

It is important to note that advertising data and its use is inextricably linked to user identity and privacy. These topics are explored separately in the following chapters.

Advertising data basics

To kick off this chapter, we will look at basic data classifications based on source, creation methods, categories and ownership. These classifications are commonly used across the industry, and it's very useful to have a firm grasp of their meaning.

Data sources

Data used in digital marketing and advertising comes from several distinct sources[32]. Website data is perhaps the most prevalent, but other common sources include mobile apps, ad campaigns, analytics tools, CRM systems, or email. Naturally, this is not a complete list - each ecosystem participant will have access to different data sources, whether first-party or external, modern or more traditional.

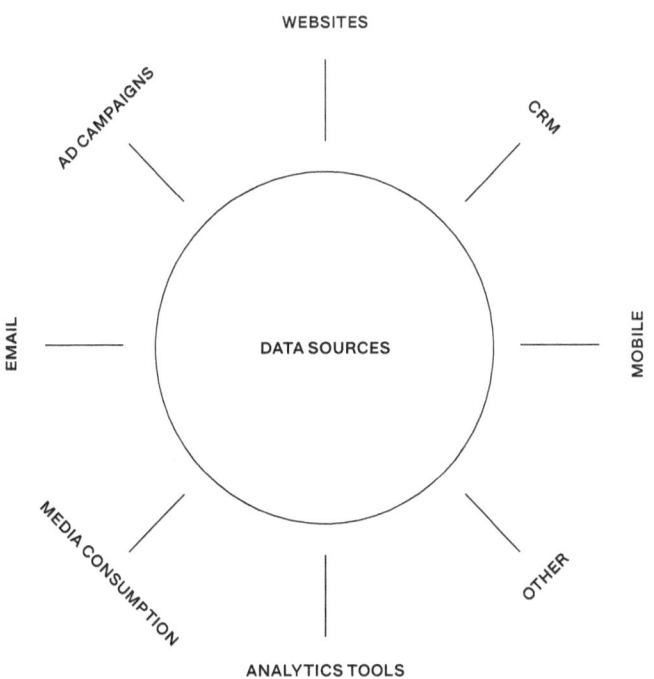

FIGURE 6: COMMON DATA SOURCES

WEBSITES

A large portion of all data used in digital advertising is gathered from websites, as data collection is relatively easy to implement at scale and offers valuable insights into user interest, intent and characteristics. This data is often collected from owned web properties or purchased from 2-nd or 3-rd parties. With recent changes to the privacy and identity landscape (e.g. gradual deprecation of third-party cookies, GDPR in the European Union), website data is increasingly more difficult to collect and share within the advertising ecosystem.

Website data can be grouped into three buckets - content/behavior related, declared, and technical data.

As users browse a website, they leave a trace of behavioral data signals which can be collected and used. This includes standard signals such as website URL, page title, page keywords, on-site search keywords, page referrer, search keyword used to get to the website, or user ID (e.g. hashed email address) if available. E-commerce websites might include additional signals, like items added to a shopping cart, products viewed, category viewed, or order value. In fact, any user interest, behavior or characteristic which can be gleaned from their website visit can be turned into a custom data signal. For example, publishers might use semantic analysis to produce high-quality custom signals related to page content (as a proxy to user interest).

Declared data is commonly gathered on websites via registration forms, sweepstakes, questionnaires, web applications, purchase events or preference settings. Technical data relates to the device used to visit a website. Signals include things like web browser, operating system, device or device type, language or geographic location.

MOBILE
When it comes to mobile, there are two common sources of data - mobile apps and mobile websites.

Mobile apps used to be a treasure trove of behavioral data, which could be easily tied to user advertising IDs (IDFA or Identifier for Advertisers on iOS, AAID/GAID or Google Advertising ID on Android). This would include data points such as app ID, session length, days since last use, hour of day the app was launched, device resolution, carrier, geo location, actions/events within the app (e.g. purchases, clicks, searches, video plays, social shares, etc.), as well as diagnostic events (such as launches, crashes, upgrades) or number of engaged users in a chosen time period. Access to mobile app data is becoming more restricted recently due to privacy measures, both on iOS (AppTracking Transparency Framework) and Android (Privacy Sandbox).

Mobile websites offer similar data to desktop websites but are often more difficult to track due to high market share of iOS devices in many countries.

ADVERTISING CAMPAIGNS

Advertising campaigns are a great source of data, both for advertisers as well as other ecosystem players who might have access to it. Key data signals include impressions, clicks, conversions (such as leads, form submissions, purchases, etc.) and ad interaction events (e.g. exposure duration, ad creative events). Properly tagged, running campaigns should also provide signals such as campaign IDs, creative IDs, business unit IDs or advertiser IDs.

ANALYTICS TOOLS

Website analytics tools, such as Google Analytics, are a fantastic source of data on website visitors. They help track on-site measures such as page view duration, number of pages visited, or visit recency. They can also capture some campaign and website events, including impressions, clicks, or conversions of various types. Data gathered with analytics tools can be used for a very granular visitor segmentation - either as a standalone source, or in conjunction with website data obtained by other means.

CUSTOMER RELATIONSHIP MANAGEMENT SOFTWARE

CRM software has been around for a while, and many companies use it to store customer information. This data can be brought to the digital environment and used for online applications such as ad targeting or analytics. Common CRM data includes customer names, addresses, phone numbers, email addresses, purchase history, contact history, customer segmentation, or loyalty program behavior.

EMAIL DATA

Email marketing programs (and related software) can be tapped to provide data for other digital applications. A typical use case is targeting users via a different channel based on their email marketing behavior (e.g. retargeting someone who unsubscribed from a mailing list with display ads). Email data includes subscription status, engagement behavior (email open rate, click-through rate, etc.) or conversion behavior.

MEDIA CONSUMPTION DATA

As all media becomes increasingly digitized, a rich user media consumption behavior data stream emerged. This primarily includes connected TV (and broader OTT video consumption), but also audio (music, podcasts, radio etc.) or books (read on electronic devices).

OTHER DATA SOURCES

There are many other data sources which can be used for digital marketing and advertising. These range from established sources with offline origins (e.g. public and private records, databases, surveys or census data), through various panels and point of sale records all the way to modern, cutting-edge data streams (including for instance wearables, beacons, connected internet-of-things devices or marketing automation platforms). As long as it can be matched to a digital user profile, digital ID or device of any kind, any data point can be useful for ad targeting or other applications.

Data creation methods

Depending on how data was created, it can be classified as declared, inferred or modelled. Declared data (sometimes referred to as zero-party data, as explained later in this chapter) is given by the users themselves, and might include things such as age, gender, social graph (friends and family), interests and so on. Facebook is a treasure trove of declared data, from user profiles to things they like or share. Declared data is commonly collected from registration forms, or by running sweepstakes. Inferred data is not given by the users directly but is deduced – usually from their behavior. Someone reading a lot of computer game reviews is likely to be interested in playing computer games. Finally, modelled data uses a large data set to find users matching a desired profile. Typical application is look-a-like modelling, where an algorithm tries to find users who are similar to a given user group.

Data categories

Common user-related data categories used for ad targeting include demographics, interest, intent, and lifestyle[33]. Other interesting data categories include B2B, location, advertising, privacy, and identity data.

Demographic and socio-economic data includes characteristics like gender, age, life status (single, married, with children, retired, etc.), wealth, income, financial behavior or health.

Interest data is typically inferred from user behavior, and often uses weaker but frequent data signals for classification compared to intent data. For example, someone reading a lot of photography content might be classified as having an interest in photography. Special interest data types include media consumption preferences, seasonal or event-based data, or political inclination.

Like interest data, intent data is also commonly derived from user behavior. However, data signals for this classification are typically much stronger, more specific, and sufficiently recent. To illustrate, someone visiting a price comparison site, searching for a "Fujifilm X100V" and reading several reviews has a very likely intent of purchasing one. While the bulk of intent data is purchase intent, there are other intent sub-categories - such as voting, moving, or service cancellation.

Lifestyle is a broad and relatively vague category, based on clusters of users with similar profiles. Clustering is commonly done in an automated fashion - algorithms are used on pools of raw data to find groups of users similar to each other, but distinct enough from the other groups. These groups (or clusters) are then given descriptions by human analysts to make them usable and marketable. Clustering can be done on general user data (resulting in "Lifestyle" segments, such as "Urban Yuppies" or "Soccer Moms"), or more specific data pools (to create financial, psychographic or other segmentation).

B2B data tends to be singled out, as it uses specific data sources that are not widely available. B2B data is user-related, focusing on business professionals in their respective roles. Two sub-categories are common - firmographics and B2B intent. Firmographics describe the type of organization a user is working for and their role (industry, size, revenue, function, level, etc.). B2B intent data looks at intent signals in business context - whether it's business software purchase, renting out office space, or taking out a business loan. Beyond generic B2B data, some high-value segments (such as healthcare professionals) have their own data segments and providers.

Location data can be used to build unique geo-behavioral segments. These are often based on known locations of points of interest, and users' movement (including dwell time, frequency, etc.) around them. For example, if someone frequently visits shopping malls and spends a lot of time there, they can be classified as an avid shopper. Location segments can be based around activities, intent or even brand preferences (e.g. loyal Starbucks customer).

Advertising data is generated by and related to advertising campaigns. Common data points include impressions, clicks and conversions. This data is important for campaign efficiency and evaluation.

Privacy data has come to the fore in the recent years, particularly following the introduction of General Data Protection Regulation (GDPR) in the European Union. Privacy data includes signals indicating users' privacy preferences (e.g. Transparency Consent String).

Finally, identity data is extremely interesting - its primary use case is building identity graphs of users, their devices and other related data. To illustrate, an identity data signal might include a combination of cookie ID and hashed email, both related to the same user. By combining many similar signals, a company might be able to build a comprehensive profile of user's cookies, IDs (email addresses, phone numbers, etc.) and other identifiers. At scale, an identity graph of millions of users can serve for cross-device/browser/platform ad targeting, frequency capping, measurement, attribution and other applications. Identity data generation and application has been heavily influenced by recent privacy and identity changes, as will be discussed in separate chapters.

Data ownership

A final categorization of data used in digital advertising is based on ownership, and we can distinguish zero-, first-, second-, and third-party data. This distinction is from the perspective of a single ecosystem participant (e.g. user, advertiser, publisher, etc.).

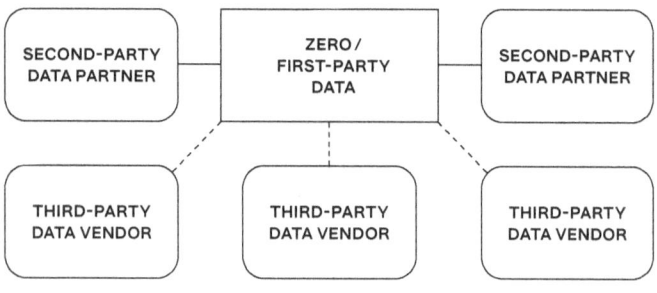

FIGURE 7: DATA CATEGORIZATION BY OWNERSHIP

FIRST-PARTY DATA

First-party data is collected directly from owned or controlled sources, typically by advertisers or publishers[34]. This is the most valuable, exclusive and accurate data marketers have (and it's free, apart from the technology costs). For example, an e-commerce site can collect data on its visitors, including products they viewed, put into a shopping basket, or purchased. From this data, they can determine purchase intent or other behavioral patterns, and personalize their marketing approach for each visitor.

As great as first-party data is, limited scale is a major downside. For an e-commerce player to obtain such data, users must first visit their website, mobile app or other directly controlled property. Only a fraction of their potential customers does, so other methods must be used to reach out to the rest. First-party data use can be also limited due to legal reasons, particularly in the European Union. It must be handled and used in line with privacy laws, as well as any user agreements that were made at the time of data collection.

SECOND-PARTY DATA

Second-party data is obtained through partnerships with other entities and is basically their first-party data. To illustrate, a price comparison site might share their first-party customer data with an e-commerce site. To the e-commerce site, this is second-party data – and is indeed very valuable. Often, partners would mutually share their first-party data to gain a better user understanding. Second-party data sharing can also take the form of data co-ops, where multiple partners (typically publishers) pool their data together.

Given the quality and uniqueness of second-party data, it is in high demand. To many data owners, such as small, specialized publishers, providing their valuable data to close partners can open a new revenue stream. A downside for all parties is the need to maintain data-sharing partnerships, and potential data leaks if partners are unreliable. Data rights and privacy issues are even more critical when providing data to other parties. First-party data often can't be shared unless user consent to do so is obtained in advance. Finally, due to the changes to identity landscape (deprecation of third-party cookies in particular), it is no longer technologically easy to share second-party data.

THIRD-PARTY DATA

Third-party data is data obtained from external providers, with no direct partnership with the buyer. For example, a publisher data sharing co-op can segment visitors based on their browsing behavior and sell these segments to advertisers for campaign targeting. To the advertiser, these segments (say car purchase intenders or photography buffs) constitute third-party data. Such data can be very useful in efficiently extending advertising campaigns to wider audiences of potential customers.

Third-party data used to be widely used, mainly for ad targeting. With the increased privacy regulation and third-party cookie deprecation, the heyday of third-party data is likely over. Some of the advantages include easy access, large scale, and increased return on advertising investment. Demand-side platforms typically integrated audience segments from several providers, and these could be easily added to any campaign. The main reason for using third-party data is an increase in advertising ROI at scale, particularly if the source is reputable and data is of high quality.

ZERO-PARTY DATA

Zero-party data, a recently prominent category of data based on ownership, is data that is intentionally shared by the users themselves. Some examples of zero-party data include communication preferences, personal context (e.g. garment size supplied to a fashion retailer), or purchase intentions. Unlike first-party data, zero-party data are declared and not inferred. Zero-party data is regarded as the highest quality but requires a lot of trust on the users' part. There's been a lot of buzz around zero-party data, for two reasons in particular. Firstly, they could to some extent replace third-party data. And secondly, new business models could become viable, based on total user control and monetization of their own data.

Advertising data ecosystem

An entire ecosystem has emerged around digital advertising data, driven by development in data collection, usage and monetization possibilities[35]. Advertisers and agencies create most of the data demand, while publishers, closed advertising platforms and third-party vendors/data exchanges provide data supply. With the demise of third-party cookies, publishers (with their own first-party data) are poised to replace third-party vendors as primary data providers within the open programmatic ecosystem.

A host of data-related solutions, services and tools exist to help with various stages of data flow. Data management platforms and more recently customer data platforms often serve as central data hubs, aided in data collection by website analytics, onboarding vendors, and tag management solutions. Data activation, especially for ad targeting, is the domain of technologies including demand-side platforms and specialized retargeting vendors, supported by dedicated ad servers and ad measurement solutions.

It is important to keep in mind that with the rapid privacy and identity changes, the entire advertising data ecosystem is undergoing major shifts. The main ones include lower general availability of data, much less interoperability among ecosystem players, shift of control over data to the sell-side (namely closed advertising ecosystems and publishers) and certain technology vendors (browsers and operating systems) to the detriment of buy side, and more control and transparency for internet users. Some of the key participants in the programmatic advertising data ecosystem include advertisers, publishers, closed advertising platforms, data vendors and data management/customer data platforms.

Advertisers

Advertisers (and agencies on their behalf) create the bulk of data demand, mainly with ad targeting in mind. With the right data, they can significantly increase advertising return on investment and build very sophisticated, personalized communication strategies. Performance advertisers are heavy users of data, especially if it signals strong purchase intent (popular tactics are keyword-based search advertising or retargeting). Brand advertisers can also take advantage of data (such as user interest or sociodemography) to reach their desired target group. Beyond ad targeting, advertisers can use data for analytics, user profiling, modeling, website customization and other applications. Changes in identity landscape, discussed in a later chapter, mean that advertisers will become more reliant on publishers and closed advertising ecosystems for their data needs.

Publishers

Publishers, with their web properties and mobile apps, are a major source of digital advertising data. User behavior on these properties can be tracked - either by publishers or third parties. Publishers can implement and manage data collection technology themselves or allow an external partner (typically a data vendor) to do it on their behalf. One of the primary reasons for publishers to collect data is the extra revenue it can bring when activated on the publisher inventory or sold to interested parties. Publishers also often use the data for other purposes than advertising, such as content customization, website optimization or analytics.

Closed advertising platforms

Facebook, Google/YouTube, Instagram, LinkedIn, Twitter, TikTok and other advertising platforms thrive on data. With hundreds of millions of active users, they have unparalleled access to high-quality interest, intent or sociodemographic data. These platforms offer efficient and relatively easy to use one-stop digital advertising solutions on their properties. Due to data scale, quality identity graphs based on user login, along with user attention and other factors, closed advertising platforms have proven wildly popular with advertisers and agencies.

Data vendors and exchanges

Hundreds of specialized data vendors, as well as several major data exchanges, have built a business around collecting, processing and selling data for ad targeting and other purposes. Many are widely integrated across the ecosystem, enabling them to easily transfer data to DMPs, demand side platforms, ad servers, content management systems, analytics platforms and elsewhere. However, due to the deprecation of third-party cookies in web browsers and privacy regulation, it is increasingly difficult to not only collect data by third-party vendors, but primarily to transmit it across the ecosystem.

Data Management Platforms and Customer Data Platforms

Data management platform (DMP) is a complex piece of software used to collect, store, classify, analyze and manage large quantities of data from various sources including web sites, mobile apps, CRM systems or external data partners. DMPs are often used by advertisers and publishers, but also by some agencies. DMPs were originally built primarily around third-party cookie IDs, but due to their demise need to pivot towards first-party IDs and user identifiers such as email addresses or phone numbers. DMPs are now challenged by a relatively recent category, the so-called customer data platforms (CDPs). CDPs are built around real users and their profiles, rather than legacy device/browser identifiers (cookies, device IDs, etc.). As such, CDPs offer a more future-proof solution, albeit with some scale and data activation possibilities restrictions compared to traditional DMPs.

Data activation

With basic data classification and overview of the ecosystem out of the way, let's look at how data is used in digital advertising. We'll focus on ad targeting here, but please note that other use cases for data exist in programmatic, including measurement or campaign optimization.

When it comes to ad targeting, it is important to distinguish prospecting and retargeting. Retargeting means reaching out to users the advertiser already knows, whereas prospecting means looking for potential customers an advertiser doesn't know yet. A sound strategy is to attract potential new shoppers through a prospecting campaign aimed at relevant audience segments or the right context. Once such prospects show interest and visit the advertiser website, they can be communicated with very efficiently through retargeting. A good media planner (whether in-house or at an agency) should be able to combine the right prospecting and retargeting tactics, to achieve optimal return on investment.

Prospecting

To communicate with new potential customers an advertiser doesn't know yet, several prospecting tactics can be incorporated into an overall strategy. In this section, we will explore some of them, including contextual targeting, behavioral targeting, and look-a-like modeling.

CONTEXTUAL TARGETING

Website content (or website audience profile, if known) has traditionally been used to target advertising, based on presumed overlap with advertisers' potential customers. For example, if the content of a site is based around childcare, an advertiser can expect to be able to target an audience of mums there. A media planner would select a portfolio of sites where the advertiser's audience can be reached, and their campaign would run there. This method of targeting has been gaining renewed popularity in the recent years, as it doesn't require either cookies or user consent. There's also been a significant progress in terms of targeting accuracy, particularly due to the rise of semantic targeting.

Contextual targeting relies on scanning web pages for specific keywords, to estimate relevance of a page to an advertiser's target group. Keywords or categories are chosen by an advertiser (or their agency), and ads are served on matching pages. This method of targeting is very common, given the relative precision and ease of implementation (many advertisers have fine-tuned keyword lists ready from their PPC campaigns).

There are some drawbacks to contextual targeting though. Firstly, many words have multiple meanings, so a simple scanning technology is unable to determine the exact meaning in the context where they appear. And secondly, basic contextual targeting cannot gauge overall context of a page, including sentiment or appropriateness. Such problems can be partially solved by restricting a keyword list to make it safer but doing so might limit scale of the campaign. To combat all these drawbacks, semantic targeting has come to the fore in recent years.

Semantic targeting is a more sophisticated form of contextual targeting, utilizing semantic techniques and natural language processing to determine the overall context of a page. Unlike simple contextual targeting, semantic technology can recognize the exact meaning of words on a page, as well as content topic and overall sentiment (which can be positive, neutral or negative). Compared to basic contextual targeting, semantic targeting enables larger campaign scale (particularly in bigger markets), while still maintaining relevance and brand safety.

It is important to note that not every web page is suitable for contextual targeting. Many web pages don't offer a single and clearly defined context (e.g. the main page of a news site). Here, behavioral targeting could be more appropriate.

Many industry players offer contextual targeting solutions, from specialized vendors to publishers, media agencies or demand-side platforms. Well-known contextual vendors include Peer39, GumGum or Integral Ad Science.

BEHAVIORAL TARGETING

Behavioral targeting, also known as audience targeting, relies on individual user behavioral data to increase advertising relevance. For example, if a user started frequently visiting car-related websites to read reviews and compare specs, it is reasonable to infer they are in the market for a new car. It makes sense for a car brand to target advertising to such users, increasing efficiency of their campaigns. In a win-win-win situation, users also benefit from seeing ads they might be interested in, and publishers are able to sell their targeted inventory at higher CPMs.

Behavioral targeting starts by collecting "signals", which are essentially meaningful data points with regard to user intent, interests, or profile. Such signals might include pages visited, keywords users searched for, clicks or other events users triggered, or user-related declared data. Behavioral/audience segments are then defined based on recency and frequency of relevant signals. Various signals can be assigned a different weight – searching for a particular keyword (such as "Ford dealership") could be a stronger indicator of intent than visiting a generic car-related page.

Data management platforms (DMPs) and customer data platforms (CDPs) are typically used to facilitate behavioral targeting. Segments are usually defined manually, and the resulting data quality therefore depends not only on the quality of signals, but also on choices made in segment definition. These choices include factors like signal recency, frequency, or strength. For some segments, data quality can be increased through shorter recency windows – this is typically the case with segments capturing purchase intent. Someone searching for "Ford dealership" yesterday is more likely to be in-market than if the search happened a month ago. For other segments, such as those capturing interest, long recency windows along with higher signal frequency requirement might be more appropriate. Another common design choice is the balance of stronger and weaker signals in segment definition – while using only very strong signals improves data quality, it might severely limit scale. Data providers typically aim for a good balance between data quality and scale, which involves a lot of trial and error to get right.

Behavioral targeting is ideal for prospecting campaigns. Advertisers often purchase third-party audience data for this purpose, either from specialized data vendors, or directly from publishers (here, advertisers are essentially purchasing publishers' first-party data, immune to third-party cookie deprecation). Behavioral data quality varies by data provider, so it always makes sense to test several targeting options. Combined with subsequent retargeting and other parts of a digital communication mix, behavioral targeting is an excellent way to acquire new customers or spread brand message.

LOOK-A-LIKE MODELING

Look-a-like modeling is a popular way of using behavioral or declared data, allowing advertisers to achieve both targeting accuracy and scale. Look-a-like modeling works by algorithmically finding users with similar behaviors or characteristics to a given user group. This process requires a very large user pool, with enough data points for each user.

An advertiser usually chooses the audience they would like to extend – the underlying segment. This could be for instance users who have converted on the advertiser's site, site visitors, users belonging to a certain audience segment, or even an e-mail list from a CRM database. The underlying segment must be a subgroup of a vendor user pool. Ideally a modeling vendor collects data on the underlying segment directly for subsequent look-a-like modeling. If an advertiser would like to use an external underlying segment (such as an e-mail list from their CRM database), this audience first needs to be matched to the user pool of a vendor. There is usually a minimum underlying segment size for a modeling algorithm to work properly.

Once the underlying segment is selected, an algorithm can look for users who are similar. Resulting quality of a look-a-like model will depend on the vendor algorithm, the quality and the scale of their data (relative to the base group), the size of the underlying segment, and other factors. It is therefore important to choose the right vendor, as results can vary greatly.

There is also typically an inverse correlation between the size of the resulting look-a-like audience and its similarity to the underlying segment. Sometimes the resulting model is either too narrow or too inaccurate to be of any use. However, look-a-like modeling can also work very well, and is a great use of behavioral or declared data to extend campaign reach.

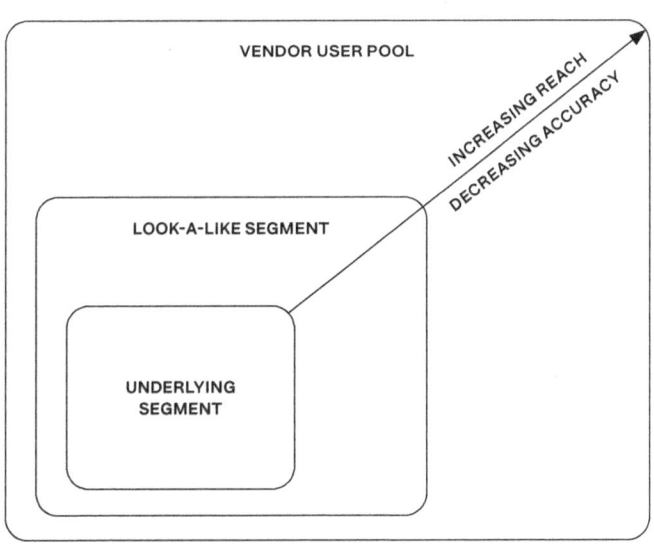

FIGURE 8: LOOK-A-LIKE MODELING

Retargeting

Retargeting is a form of behavioral targeting aimed at users an advertiser already knows. Typically, these users visited the advertiser's website, entered their loyalty program, or use their mobile app. Although retargeting technically falls under behavioral targeting, it deserves a separate section given its importance and specific role in current display advertising strategies. There is little doubt that retargeting is very effective, so much so that it has become somewhat of a mandatory item in any media plan. After all, what could possibly work better than communicating with people who have already in some way (usually by visiting your website) shown interest in your brand or product? However, with the demise of third-party cookies and stricter privacy rules, the future of retargeting is uncertain.

RETARGETING PROCESS

Retargeting can be simple, but it can also become a fairly complex endeavor. Before discussing it further, it is helpful to understand the process of simple site retargeting based on third-party cookies, using a retargeting vendor. Let's suppose an e-commerce advertiser wants to show their ads to users who put an item into a shopping basket but didn't complete a purchase. This is how the magic happens:

1. Retargeting pixel (i.e. a tracking pixel/script used for retargeting) from a chosen vendor is placed on an advertiser's website. This can include an entire website, or just selected pages (for example the basket page in case of an e-commerce site).

2. Conversion pixel from the vendor is placed on a post-conversion page, to track users who have already converted. This can be a "thank you for your purchase" page for instance. This pixel is there to ensure that visitors, who have already converted, are excluded from the retargeting campaign.

3. When a user visits advertiser's website, the retargeting pixel saves a cookie into their browser. All the users who have a cookie set (and possibly meet other criteria, such as no conversion in the last month) form a retargeting pool.

4. The vendor needs to use cookie syncing (discussed in the first chapter) or other form of data transfer with their partners, to be able to recognize bid requests related to users in the retargeting pool.

5. Retargeting vendor bids on selected requests related to users in the retargeting pool. Bidding algorithms differ with each vendor and vary in their degree

of sophistication. The vendor aims to win as many impressions as possible while maintaining high efficiency.

6. As users in a retargeting pool browse the web, they see ads the retargeting vendor has purchased on behalf of an advertiser. If they make a conversion (for example a purchase) on an advertiser's website, they are usually excluded from the retargeting pool for some time.

ADVANCED RETARGETING

This is site retargeting process in a nutshell. However, there is a lot of freedom and flexibility in how it can be set up. An advertiser can define their retargeting pool in any way, particularly if they have access to a data management platform or a customer data platform. There's no reason to use just one retargeting pool, either. An advertiser can run a separate retargeting campaign for regular customers who haven't made a purchase in a while, and for new ones who showed interest (perhaps by making more than five page views on the site, or putting something in a shopping basket), but didn't proceed to click the buy button. Also, there is no set optimal frequency for retargeting campaigns, and it should be adjusted for each retargeting pool to achieve an optimal return – without alienating potential customers.

Dynamic retargeting is also a very common way to improve retargeting efficiency. Rather than showing the same creative to all users in the retargeting pool, the creative is personalized based on what exactly each user viewed on the advertiser's site. For example, if a user viewed a specific camera (say Fujifilm X100V) on an e-commerce site, a vendor employing dynamic retargeting would put together a creative featuring a Fujifilm X100V on the fly, in response to a bid request for this specific user. Creative is personalized automatically based on a product feed supplied by the advertiser, for all users and all impressions which are part of the dynamic retargeting campaign. The product feed contains data such as product names or images, and is commonly supplied in an .xml, .csv or .txt format.

BEYOND WEBSITE RETARGETING

So far, we have only discussed website retargeting, but other forms of retargeting exist as well, including e-mail retargeting, search retargeting, and customer list retargeting. With simple e-mail retargeting, ads are shown to users who have opened an advertiser's e-mail. Search retargeting is a tactic where users who have searched for selected keywords are retargeted.

Increasingly popular is retargeting using lists of customer e-mail addresses and other identifiers, such as phone numbers. This is sometimes referred to as CRM or customer list retargeting. An advertiser simply uploads an e-mail list (provided users consented to this) from their database to a vendor, who matches the e-mail addresses to user cookies or profiles (with varying match rates depending on the vendor). These users can then be retargeted as if they had visited the advertiser site.

Chapter 6
Identity

Identity and privacy are the new battlefronts of programmatic advertising, making for yet another revolution that is set to transform the industry. The new dividing lines will be drawn around access to stable and consented user identity, favoring walled gardens to the detriment of an open ecosystem. While it is hard to predict the impact of identity and privacy changes at the time of writing, one thing is clear - big players, particularly those controlling end-to-end ad tech stacks and user relationships, are best placed to cope with and profit from these changes. Smaller publishers and advertisers relying on third-party technologies and data for targeting, measurement or monetization will be hurt the most. Further consolidation and lower interoperability within the industry can be expected, hopefully made up for by more privacy control and data protection of internet users.

Identity

Let us start with some definitions to outline a context for further discussion. What does identity actually mean?

An identifier could be more formally defined as a means of consistently recognizing a specific entity as distinct from others across multiple interactions[36]. When identity is discussed in the digital advertising industry, people tend to talk about user identity and related identifiers. One or more identifiers of the same user comprise their identity. It is important to note that in the programmatic ecosystem, an identifier doesn't always identify an actual human user - often it's an identifier of a device or a browser. Nevertheless, even this proxy identity has brought tremendous efficiency and value to the industry.

Why is identity important?

In a nutshell, user identity is the cornerstone of efficient digital advertising. It enables the pairing of otherwise unrelated events together to a single user, creating a long-term event log, and using this data to make advertising ever more efficient in delivering desired outcomes. These events include everything from page views, ad impressions, clicks, dwell times, interactions, video play times to conversions and payments. Broad access to identity and related data has enabled programmatic advertising to become one of the most efficient channels for advertisers and agencies, while offering generous inventory monetization to publishers.

Many common use cases that make for an overall efficient advertising ecosystem rely on some form of user identity. These include behavioral targeting, retargeting, frequency capping, or measurement (e.g. conversions, ROI, reach or frequency). In turn, subsequent optimization of advertising campaigns or publisher monetization strategies is dependent on identity as well.

While by no means perfect, the legacy identity ecosystem based on third-party cookies provided a fairly equal and accessible baseline for all ad tech players on which to build and improve efficiency. Due to third-party cookie deprecation in browsers, alternative approaches are taking over. Consented authenticated identity in particular is on a qualitatively much higher level - enabling more precise linking of user-related events across more digital environments for a longer time. On the other hand, contextual advertising will lack this data layer enabling increasing efficiency. It remains to be seen which players will gain or retain access to identity and at what level of quality - this will determine their long-term competitiveness and shape the programmatic advertising landscape.

Legacy identity ecosystem

The programmatic advertising ecosystem has been historically built around identity based on third-party cookies. To understand how the demise of third-party cookies created an identity crisis, it helps to understand how the legacy identity ecosystem works. A server of **ad technology A** would set and maintain a third-party cookie in every browser (client) that sends requests to it. The cookie would contain a unique identifier per browser (note not per user, as a single user might use several browsers), since a server with access to cookies across various domains and browsers could ensure it didn't assign duplicate IDs. In effect, **ad technology A** would create its own browser-level identity graph.

Every ad tech company did the same thing, generating a multitude of overlapping ID graphs. Each browser would have many third-party cookies stored, each containing a unique ID from a different ad technology. In effect, a single human user would typically have many different identifiers within the ecosystem. These IDs were then mapped to one another in a cookie syncing process described in chapter one, allowing ad tech companies to become interoperable and create an open programmatic ecosystem with mutually recognized identity. Synchronized third-party cookie based IDs enabled the various DSPs, SSPs, DMPs and other parts of the programmatic stack to understand which browser an ad was being displayed in, enabling things like targeting, frequency capping, or measurement.

To reduce the need for every ad technology to constantly synchronize IDs with all the others one by one, an idea of a universal ID emerged. The concept was simple - each ad technology would only synchronize their ID with a common universal ID, which would then be used and recognized around the ecosystem. The proposition was gaining traction, spearheaded by DigiTrust ID by IAB Tech Lab and several competing solutions by The Trade Desk, ID5 or the Advertising ID Consortium. However, this original concept of a universal ID relied on third-party cookies for synchronization. With the rapid deprecation of third-party cookies by web browsers, universal ID stopped making sense before ever reaching industry-wide scale.

PROS AND CONS OF THIRD-PARTY COOKIE BASED IDENTITY

Identity based on third-party cookies, albeit not perfect, enabled the emergence and growth of an open and competitive programmatic ecosystem. Each ad technology was free to create a scaled proprietary ID graph and synchronize it with partners of their own choosing. There was a low barrier to entry into the industry when it comes to identity, promoting competition and innovation. The user experience, at least prior to privacy regulation, was great in the sense that it was possible to browse around the open web with no need to log in or pay a subscription fee. Third-party cookie based identity also partially (by no means perfectly) protected user privacy, as the identifiers were tied to browsers rather than users, and generally had short lifespan. Publishers were able to generally support themselves with relatively high CPMs thanks to smooth targeting and measurement data flow underpinning the ecosystem. Advertisers and agencies could build their own custom technology stacks from different vendors, develop proprietary data assets and run very efficient campaigns.

However, third-party cookies were always just a workaround to generate an approximation of user identity. The most glaring issue was lack of privacy control by users - any technology with a piece of JavaScript on a website could collect and sell user data. A marketplace full of more or less scrupulous data vendors quickly emerged, triggering a need for privacy regulation. User privacy protection is often cited as the key reason for a gradual abolition of third-party cookies by browsers.

For the advertising ecosystem, third-party cookie based identity had other issues as well. To create interoperability between individual ad technologies, a complex cookie synchronization system had to be devised. This resulted in many synchronization pixels firing off on every page load, slowing websites down and requiring constant maintenance. The resulting scale of synchronized identity varied between technology stacks - some ad tech vendors had high match rates between their IDs, while others didn't. The more vendors involved in a stack (say a DSP, SSP, DMP etc.), the lower the overall match rate and scale.

Another issue was created by the relatively short lifespan of third-party cookies, resulting in inefficiency and user ID and data fragmentation. Short cookie lifespan meant that a single browser would generate many ever-changing IDs per ad technology, requiring the ecosystem to process way more IDs and related data than a number representative of actual real users. Everything from data storage and processing, targeting, campaign optimization to measurement was less efficient and accurate as a result.

Finally, with the emergence of user privacy regulation (particularly GDPR in the European Union and CCPA in California), privacy settings would often be tied to a cookie-based ID. This is not a user-friendly solution, as it typically requires the setting and maintenance of privacy settings individually across every domain or data controller the user encounters while browsing the web.

Evolution of user identity

With the demise of third-party cookies first in Safari, followed by Firefox and Edge and eventually Google Chrome (planned for the second half of 2023 at the time of writing), identity landscape changed dramatically. User identity went from a practically free commodity to an exclusive asset in just a few years, transforming the entire industry. In early 2022, it is not yet clear how exactly third-party cookie based identity will be replaced, but the most likely scenario is a combination of several approaches. These include login-based IDs, first-party cookie based IDs, new solutions to use cases that relied on identity, browser offerings, and inevitably working with partial unavailability of user identity within the digital advertising ecosystem.

FIRST-PARTY COOKIE IDS

As browsers gradually shut down support for third-party cookies, first-party cookies remained largely untouched. As discussed in chapter one, these cookies can only be set and read by a server on the same domain as the domain a user is directly visiting. This means that it is still possible to create a cookie-based identity graph, but it is limited to a single domain. For each domain there can be a separate ID graph, but unfortunately with no direct way of ID synchronization akin to third-party cookie syncing workflow. Moreover, ad technologies are reliant on publishers for access to these first-party cookie IDs. Nevertheless, first-party cookie IDs have value for the programmatic ecosystem.

The main advantages of first-party cookie IDs include potential scale, longevity, and publisher control. When it comes to scale with regards to the entire ecosystem, it is naturally far smaller than identity based on third-party cookies. But compared to the remaining alternatives, in some scenarios scale offered by first-party IDs can be sufficient and attractive. The potential is two-fold - scale within large domains/publishers, and scale achieved through probabilistic and deterministic ID matching. An ID graph created for a large domain can by itself be attractive enough for certain advertisers and ad technologies, with campaigns restricted exclusively to this domain. Moreover, first-party cookie IDs can be to some extent matched across domains using probabilistic (based on IP address, geo location, user agent and similar signals) or deterministic (based for example on user login) methods. The second advantage of first-party cookie IDs is their longevity, surviving significantly longer in web browsers compared to third-party cookies. And finally, first-party cookies and IDs stored in them are fully within publisher control, preventing covert misuse by nefarious players.

AUTHENTICATED IDENTITY

Another interesting alternative to third-party cookie based IDs for the open programmatic ecosystem is identity built on user authentication. This requires users to log in across different domains, establishing a distinct and shared identity based on their email address, phone number or another stable and unique identifier. Identity based on authentication has many benefits both for users and the ecosystem.

Firstly, such identity can be easily tied to a user profile, complete with their privacy preferences. Privacy preferences no longer need to be stored in a cookie or another temporary storage, but become permanent, transparent and easy to manage by users. Whenever a user logs in, their privacy preferences can be transferred and respected, making for a superior experience. Second, authenticated identity is a vast improvement on legacy third party cookies in terms of universality and longevity. Cookie-based IDs were limited to and fragmented by browsers, while logins establish a single identity across all browsers and devices of an individual user. As users tend to keep their email addresses, phone numbers or other identifiers for a long time, the resulting identity can span years. This longevity combined with universality and user privacy control elevates authenticated user identity to a qualitatively whole new level for the industry, enabling new propositions and workflows.

Scale of authenticated user identity is a major drawback though, particularly within the open programmatic ecosystem. The requirement for users to log in is a major hurdle, both from UX and publisher preparedness perspective. National and global efforts are under way to standardize and normalize user authentication and make the resulting identity usable in programmatic while respecting and protecting user privacy. Such initiatives include European Net ID in Germany, Czech Ad ID in the Czech Republic or Unified ID 2.0 on a global scale.

ALTERNATIVE APPROACHES

With third-party cookies, user identity - albeit not perfect - underpinned many of the use cases which have become standard in the programmatic advertising industry. Behavioral targeting, retargeting, frequency capping or measurement (e.g. conversions, frequency, reach) all relied on third-party cookies. With their demise, along with stricter privacy regulation and a rise in the usage of AdBlock, alternative approaches are needed to account for the portion of traffic lacking usable identity or user consent.

Many of the measurement use cases are increasingly augmented through data modeling. For example, a portion of conversions is obscured to DSPs due to either lack of user identity to tie them back to impressions and clicks, or a consent to do so. Although these conversions occur and generate revenue for advertisers, they simply cannot be directly measured and reported. This is where modeling comes in - the missing portion of conversions is estimated, with the aim of bringing DSP reporting more in line with reality and enabling better campaign optimization. Similarly, campaign reach or impression frequency can be modeled, where accurate measurement isn't possible. Such data modeling is a standard practice across the industry but has its issues. Each ad technology has their own approach, which leads to a lack of standardization and transparency. Advertisers in theory get more accurate data compared to no modeling at all, but they lose some degree of control.

When it comes to behavioral targeting, a common alternative approach is switching from using third-party data to reliance on publisher first-party data. End of third-party cookie support in browsers spells the demise of traditional data vendors and related marketplace. Instead, behavioral targeting data is increasingly supplied by large publishers, who have the scale to make it worthwhile. For some publishers, this means developing the expertise and technical capability - but the opportunity is significant. As for advertisers, this trend is both good and bad. On the plus side, first-party data comes from clear sources and advantageous data deals can be negotiated easier in a more fragmented ecosystem. Unfortunately, fragmentation can mean the necessity to combine several first-party data sources to achieve enough campaign scale.

In the light of third-party cookie deprecation and privacy restrictions particularly in Europe, contextual targeting came back into favor. With advances including semantic analysis or video recognition, contextual targeting is better than ever before. It offers an alternative to first-party data, providing greater campaign scale and cross-publisher reach. However, not all content is suitable for contextual targeting, and targeting efficiency often lags behind behavioral advertising.

BROWSER SOLUTIONS

With the gradual deprecation of third-party cookies by Safari, Mozilla Firefox, Microsoft Edge and eventually Google Chrome, web browsers themselves offer replacement for some of the use cases that relied on them. At the time of writing, the discussion centers mainly around Google Chrome. Chrome promises a set of solutions/ APIs under an umbrella name "Privacy Sandbox." These should offer alternative ways to accomplish for example conversion measurement, campaign targeting, or retargeting without third-party cookies. In fact, Chrome doesn't require any kind of replacement identity on the side of ad technologies and publishers. It remains to be seen how valuable these solutions will be for the ecosystem, with other players being wary of ceding too much control to browsers, particularly the dominant one. Nevertheless, browser solutions to advertising use cases will most likely become a standard part of programmatic platforms.

Chapter 7
Privacy

Online privacy is a very complex topic, involving intricate technical, legal, competitive and ethical aspects. Particularly in recent years, privacy has become a focal point of fierce industry competition - various players use it to differentiate and market their offerings, strengthen their competitive position or steer related legislation in a desired direction. Meanwhile, regulators are working to boost user digital privacy protection across various jurisdictions. At the heart of the current privacy topic prominence is the possibility to collect personal data on an unprecedented scale, enabled by rapid digitalization of many aspects of human existence. Common activities like internet browsing, social media and web application use, online communication as well as wearing of smart devices can all leave a digital trace. This data can be collected, stored and analyzed, and is often used for marketing or security purposes.

Personal data is a precious asset, especially if the information is unique, valuable, on a large scale and collected over a long period of time. Most of this data is collected and controlled by relatively few private companies and can be potentially accessed by government agencies as well. A privacy controversy arises from the fact that the general public has limited knowledge of this practice, and little control over their personal data.

From the user perspective, some level of privacy has been lost or given up, often without conscious consent. Many online services ask users to grant data ownership generated by using the service to the service provider, in exchange for free access. This trade-off can be justified by subsequent data utilization to make the service better, or monetization helping to fund the service. However, users frequently agree to terms of use without reading or thoroughly understanding them and are unaware of the value exchange they are making. Similarly, even in jurisdictions requiring special user consent (e.g. GDPR in the European Union), users often don't grasp the full weight of the consent they are giving. The extent to which users are consciously willing to trade their personal data for free services therefore remains questionable.

From the marketer perspective, user data can significantly improve the efficiency and the quality of customer relationships. Data ownership or access constitutes an unquestionable competitive advantage, enabling a whole new level of communication targeting and relationship management. But marketers need to be careful – privacy concerns can lead to erosion of trust, with potentially grave consequences.

Privacy regulation

Privacy regulation is key in shaping the programmatic ecosystem towards better protection of user data, while at the same time enabling competition and innovation. It is important to set fundamental, and if possible stable rules for the data economy, to build consumer trust and define a clear playing field for the industry.

The European Union has been at the forefront of user privacy protection and regulation. Most notably the General Data Protection Regulation (GDPR), which came into effect on May 25th, 2018, offers high transparency and privacy control standards for EU residents. Another prominent EU privacy law is the ePrivacy Directive, to be superseded by a very controversial ePrivacy Regulation. Due to the profound impact of GDPR, ePrivacy Directive and potentially ePrivacy Regulation on digital advertising industry data practices, more detailed overviews of the regulations follow later in this chapter.

Although there's no federal privacy legislation in the United States akin to EU's GDPR, individual states have passed their own laws to protect user privacy. California's Consumer Privacy Act (CCPA), along with California Online Privacy Protection Act (CalOPPA) are prime examples. Additional pieces of government regulation in the USA include Electronic Communications Privacy Act (ECPA), Children's Online Privacy Protection

Act (COPPA), or Children's Internet Protection Act (CIPA).

In addition to governmental regulation, industry self-regulatory practices have been developed to promote trust, knowledge, and control of individuals with regard to digital advertising industry. The Digital Advertising Alliance Self-Regulatory Program is the most prominent and will be looked at in more detail below.

General Data Protection Regulation

General Data Protection Regulation (GDPR) is regulation aimed at strengthening and harmonizing data protection in the EU, enforceable from May 25th, 2018. It applies to both EU companies, as well as foreign companies processing data of EU residents - hence, it has a profound impact on digital advertising data ecosystem.

GDPR requires that any data processing is lawful (i.e. meeting at least one of specified conditions)[37]. Majority of digital advertising data must be processed based on explicit consent of the data subject. Record of the consent must be kept, including the exact wording, date and means of obtaining it. Special protection is awarded to children under 16 years old - consent from their parents or guardians is required. Conditions for obtaining consent are relatively strict, including for example:

- request for consent must be prominent and easy to understand
- positive opt in which requires action (no default pre-ticked boxes)
- consent can't be a precondition of service
- consent must be easy to withdraw
- purpose of data processing needs to be declared
- all organizations relying on the consent must be named

As for scope, GDPR applies to personal data - any information relating to an identified or identifiable natural person[38]. Personal identifiers may include name, address, email, IP address, IDs (e.g. cookie ID, device ID), location data, photo, medical information, etc. Under GDPR, individuals have the following rights:

1. To be informed (i.e. receive fair data processing information)
2. To access (obtaining confirmation of personal data processing and access to it)
3. To rectification (if data is inaccurate or incomplete)
4. To erasure (particularly if an individual withdraws consent)
5. To restrict processing (data may be stored, but not processed)

6. To data portability (i.e. obtaining personal data and using it elsewhere)
7. To object (to data processing based on legitimate interests, for direct marketing, or for research purposes)
8. Rights in relation to automated decision making and profiling (i.e. protection against the risk of significant, automated decisions)

GDPR differentiates between data processors and data controllers. While a controller determines the purposes and means of processing personal data, processors are responsible for the processing itself. Both controllers and processors need to comply with GDPR principles and must ensure (contractually where applicable) that personal data is adequately protected - for example against unlawful/unauthorized processing or loss. Prior to any new data processing activity (including adopting new technology, risky or sensitive data processing, or user profiling), data controllers are required to carry out an impact assessment[39]. Some organizations, such as those conducting large-scale behavioral tracking used in digital advertising, need to also appoint Data Protection Officers. DPOs are responsible for compliance with GDPR and other data protection laws.

Under GDPR, international data transfer outside of the EU is restricted to make sure adequate level of protection is afforded to individuals' data. Organizations are required to report more risky data breaches, either to a supervisory authority only, or also to affected individuals.

To ensure compliance, GDPR empowers data protection authorities with the power of levying significant fines – up to € 20,000,000 or 4 per cent of a company's annual global turnover (whichever is higher)[40].

GDPR regulation, despite the cost and administrative burden it places on organizations processing data, has been generally well received by the industry. It provides more awareness and control for individuals, increasing their trust towards digital advertising industry and the publishers and services it helps to support. This regulation also increases transparency of data flow, processing, and visibility of organizations involved. Together with unification of data protection regulation across the EU, these improvements make life easier for all digital advertising industry participants.

When it comes to programmatic advertising, GDPR is implemented via the Transparency and Consent Framework (TCF) by IAB Europe[41]. The TCF standard has been evolving, and as of writing this book, is on its second iteration (TCF 2.0). GDPR-compliant consent is typically collected from users via Consent Management Platforms (CMPs), which are built by publishers or independent vendors according to the current TCF standard. Consent Management Platforms must pass a strict compliance check, and IAB Europe maintains a list of approved vendors[42]. Some of the well-known CMP vendors include OneTrust, Quantcast or the recently merged Usercentrics and Cookiebot. On a technical level, CMP generates a Transparency and Consent String (also referred to as TC string or simply consent string). According to IAB Europe, a TC String's primary purpose is to encapsulate and encode all the information disclosed to a user and the expression of their preferences for their personal data processing under the GDPR[43]. Consent string is typically stored in a cookie or on a publisher server and passed along the programmatic supply chain to inform all relevant players about user privacy preferences. One downside of the current implementation of GDPR using the TCF is the enormous administrative burden placed on users, were they to actually carefully manage their privacy preferences across the web[44].

ePrivacy Directive and ePrivacy Regulation

Directive on privacy and electronic communications (Directive 2002/58/EC, commonly known as ePrivacy Directive), regulates several aspects of the digital advertising industry, including use of cookies.

The ePrivacy Directive mandates that "to store information or to gain access to information stored in the terminal equipment of a subscriber or user is only allowed on condition that the subscriber or user concerned is provided with clear and comprehensive information… about the purposes of the processing and is offered the right to refuse such processing by the data controller." Consent is thus generally required when using cookies for data collection and other digital advertising purposes. Consent acquisition is typically implemented via (omnipresent and immensely unpopular) cookie banners.

ePrivacy Directive, albeit controversial, is still relatively mild compared to the proposed ePrivacy Regulation which might replace it. As of writing of this book, the legislative process hasn't been completed, so final provisions and enforcement date isn't clear.

California Consumer Privacy Act

California Consumer Privacy Act (CCPA) is a relatively new piece of legislation (passed in 2018 and effective from 2020), with the aim of strengthening user privacy protection in California. The main goal is to provide consumers with more control over the personal information[49] that businesses collect about them. Among other rights, California consumers have the right to know about the personal information a business collects about them and how it is used and shared, the right to delete this information, the right to opt-out from the sale of it and a right to non-discrimination for exercising their CCPA rights. Any information that identifies, relates to, or could reasonably be linked with a consumer or their household is considered personal. This includes not only a name, social security number, or an email address, but also less intuitive data such as purchase history or internet browsing history[45].

California Online Privacy Protection Act

The California Online Privacy Protection Act (CalOPPA) regulates collection of personally identifiable information of California residents. It applies to data collection both on website and online services, as well as via mobile apps. Personally identifiable information includes data such as name, address, phone number, Social Security number, or any other information that permits a specific individual to be contacted physically or online[46]. Under CalOPPA, a prominent privacy policy must be displayed[47]. Here, users can find out for example what PII categories are being collected, or which third parties might have access to the data.

In addition, CalOPPA also regulates visitor behavioral tracking across websites and mobile apps. Privacy policy must state how the organization responds to "Do Not Track" signals from users' web browsers, or whether third parties may collect their personally identifiable information[48].

Children's Online Privacy Protection Act (COPPA)

COPPA is a US federal law, regulating online collection of personal information of children under 13 years old. It applies not only to data collection on websites directed to children, but also via online services including mobile apps and general-audience websites if they know they are collecting children's personal information. Under COPPA, website operators are required to have a prominent privacy policy. A child's participation in a game, contest, or other activity cannot depend on the child's disclosing more personal information than is reasonably necessary to participate in the activity. They also need to obtain verifiable parental consent prior to collecting children's personal information, and allow parents to access, delete, and opt out of collecting such data. Confidentiality, security and integrity of children's data must be maintained[50].

Self-regulation

In addition to external regulation, the industry is working on simultaneous self-regulation. There's a Self-Regulatory Program for Online Behavioral Advertising backed by the Interactive Advertising Bureau (IAB),

Association of National Advertisers (ANA), American Association of Advertising Agencies (4A's) the Direct Marketing Association (DMA) and the Council of Better Business Bureaus (CBBB)[51]. A notable feature of this program is an advertising option icon to be displayed alongside online ads, giving access to data collection disclosure statement together with an opt-out option.

Digital Advertising Alliance (DAA) Self-Regulatory Program

The Digital Advertising Alliance is an independent non-profit organization formed by leading advertising and marketing trade associations including American Association of Advertising Agencies (4A's), American Advertising Federation (AAF), Association of National Advertisers (ANA), Better Business Bureau (BBB), Interactive Advertising Bureau (IAB) and the Network Advertising Initiative (NAI)[52]. The DAA oversees a self-regulatory program (also known as AdChoices) focused on responsible privacy practices in the digital advertising ecosystem, with the aim of providing consumers with more transparency and control.

The DAA has issued self-regulatory principles for several areas[53] relevant to data usage in digital advertising ecosystem. These include online behavioral advertising, multi-site data collection, mobile data collection and cross-device data usage. The DAA is also behind the common arrow-shaped AdChoices icon[54] present alongside display ads, which directs users to a page with more information and an option to opt out of data-based targeting.

Technology vendor initiatives

In addition to government and industry regulation, technology vendors started playing an increasingly important role in protecting user privacy. This is both good and bad. On the one hand, users have more transparency and control, and their behavior cannot be as easily tracked as they browse the internet or use mobile apps. On the other hand, these measures tend to favor large ad tech ecosystems (i.e. walled gardens) to the detriment of smaller publishers, advertisers and the open programmatic ecosystem.

Browsers

Internet browsers have implemented many changes and restrictions in the name of privacy over the past several years, most notably when it comes to cookies. Starting with the introduction of Intelligent Tracking Prevention (ITP) in Safari in 2017, browsers have been gradually restricting the ability of ad technologies to build identity graphs. Today, Safari not only blocks third-party cookies, but also restricts the usage of first-party cookies and various work-around technologies such as link decoration. Similarly, Mozilla Firefox and Microsoft Edge block selected third-party cookies from known trackers based on a transparent block list maintained by Disconnect, Inc[55]. As of writing of this book, Google Chrome is in the process of phasing out support for third-party cookies as well and replacing them with the so-called "Privacy Sandbox".

Operating Systems

Apple is at the forefront of implementing user privacy features right into an operating system. Intelligent Tracking Prevention (ITP), first used in Apple's Safari browser, now spans all browsers on iOS. This effectively prevents cross-site tracking on iOS using third-party cookies and other means (e.g. link decoration), even on browsers that at the time of writing of this book still support third-party cookies (primarily Google Chrome). ITP alone has a profound effect on programmatic advertising, especially in markets where iOS has significant market share (United States or United Kingdom in particular). In addition, Apple has recently started enforcing an AppTrackingTransparency (ATT) framework on iOS, requiring app developers to disclose data collection practices and to obtain user consent for tracking purposes. Together with ITP, these two measures effectively prevent programmatic advertising to function efficiently on iOS. Further privacy enhancements include for example the App Privacy Report, Hide my Email feature or the so-called iCloud Private Relay. Google also aims to bake privacy measures right into the Android operating system by integrating the Privacy Sandbox originally designed for Chrome browser[56].

Identity and Privacy

The topics of privacy and user identity are very closely related, and in tandem have a profound effect on programmatic advertising. This is simply because data is the lifeblood of programmatic - it enables precise targeting, measurement and optimization of advertising campaigns to reach their desired objectives. Access to high-quality, long-term data and the ability to process it in smart ways do deliver client efficiency is what will differentiate advertising technologies in the long run. Privacy measures are increasingly providing users with more transparency and control over how their data is collected and used, which is undoubtedly a positive and timely development. At the same time, it is becoming more difficult to collect data and to tie it back to a common user/device identifier. Unfortunately, these profound changes don't have the same impact on all industry players. Not only do bigger ad tech platforms (walled gardens in particular) have more resources to keep up with and influence regulation and browser/OS changes, but they are also in a better position to retain a key competitive advantage in the new market reality - user identity.

User identity is a key to data, which is critical for ad tech platform efficiency. The best kind of user identity at the moment is stable over time, cross-device and cross-platform, tied to a real person and privacy regulation compliant. With the demise of third-party cookies and new regulation such as GDPR or CCPA, this kind of identity (or close enough) is still achievable within large first-party ecosystems that integrate buy-side, sell-side and advertising technology. On the other hand, the open programmatic ecosystem is increasingly denied such an identity base, with replacements that will never rival high-quality identity graphs of large walled gardens in terms of scale and advertising efficiency. As of writing this book, the privacy and identity trends are pushing the industry towards consolidation in the form of closed advertising ecosystems. It remains to be seen how this plays out over time, but we might soon see an industry with less competition and higher barriers to entry. At the same time, vast repositories of long-term user data are likely to still exist, albeit controlled by only a handful of players.

User privacy is an important topic, and great progress has been made in this regard over the past several years. Users, particularly in the European Union and California, gained more control and transparency when it comes to their online data. There's still a lot to be done, and what we see today are the early days of digital privacy maturation. However, privacy protection shouldn't justify consolidation of monopoly power within the digital advertising industry. Going forward, we need smarter regulation that balances user privacy rights with competitiveness for publishers, advertisers and ad tech providers of all sizes.

Chapter 8
Emerging Media Channels

Programmatic advertising is no longer anything new. Rather, it is an established way of trading digital ad inventory including display, video, or audio. Programmatic has become standard for traditional online publishers, and the frontier of innovation is moving towards still largely untapped channels. These include perhaps most prominently connected TV, but also retail media, digital audio, or digital out-of-home. The final chapter of this book will provide a succinct introduction to these emerging media channels, which will shape the industry conversations for years to come.

Connected TV

Connected TV (CTV) has been a hot topic in programmatic advertising for a few years and will continue to drive passionate conversations going forward. The reason is simple - CTV (or rather OTT in its AVOD variant, as defined further in the text), presents a massive growth opportunity for programmatic players as TV viewing undergoes its digital revolution. This revolution is, just like in more mature programmatic channels, primarily about data. With data and per-impression programmatic buying, advertisers can target, optimize, personalize, and measure performance like never before in the history of TV. Naturally, it yet remains to be seen which players will keep control of the data, and how this will play out in the overall shift towards protecting user privacy in the digital world.

According to the Interactive Advertising Bureau, connected TV is defined as a TV that is connected to the internet via an internal device (i.e. Smart TV) or an external device (for example, Apple TV, Roku or gaming consoles). In a nutshell, video content is delivered to a TV screen through the internet[57]. This now aligns with an updated Media Rating Council view, whereby CTV is defined as the delivery of digital video to televisions via internet-connected devices (or functionality within the television itself), including both IP set-top boxes that receive signals from digital video ad servers (and widgets on them) as well as USB and HDMI multimedia devices, Smart TVs and gaming consoles that do not require set top boxes or converters[58].

A broader definition is sometimes used to encompass services enabling internet-delivered video viewing on other devices beyond TV. According to the Media

Rating Council, Over the Top (OTT) encompasses the above CTV criteria as well as non-linear video content that is delivered to a TV screen but is also available via desktop or mobile devices (i.e., streaming services)[59]. Examples of OTT services include Netflix, Amazon Prime Video, Hulu, HBO GO or Disney+.

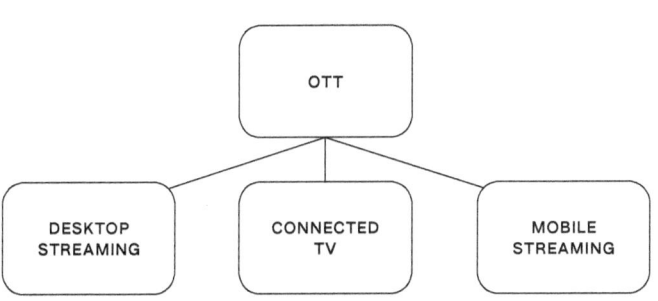

FIGURE 9: OTT VS. CONNECTED TV

Beyond the umbrella definitions of CTV and OTT, it is important to differentiate various video monetization models. Subscription video-on-demand (SVOD) enables users to access video content for a recurring subscription fee. Since users typically receive an ad-free experience, this part of the CTV market is off-limits to programmatic advertising. Well-known examples of SVOD providers include Netflix, Amazon Prime Video or Hulu. On the other hand, advertising-based video-on-demand (AVOD) offers users free access to video content in exchange for viewing ads. Users have historically preferred ad-supported business models, so this part of the market is set to grow and eventually dominate. YouTube is a typical example, along with Hulu, Sling TV or a host of smaller and local players. Finally, transactional video-on-demand (TVOD) enables users to purchase or rent individual pieces of video content for a fee.

There are many factors that make the growing CTV AVOD market attractive to advertisers. TV typically remains the biggest screen in most households, with proven effectiveness in brand building. With CTV, each user or household gets their own on-demand prime time, easing the competition from other advertisers. As this platform digitally matures, previously unavailable opportunities are opening. Advertisers can bring in targeting data and run tighter, more efficient campaigns. Although a lot of work remains to be done in this regard, measurability has vastly higher potential compared to traditional linear TV. As TV advertising becomes programmatic, advertisers gain more flexibility throughout the campaign management process. This benefits users as well, as they get more relevant and consistent advertising experience throughout their digital touchpoints.

Connected TV and programmatic trading

The programmatic ecosystem built primarily around display ads is gradually expanding into Connected TV/OTT. Buying this inventory programmatically has many advantages in the long run, such as providing a more centralized approach, enabling scale, and offering a unified view of the data used for segmentation, measurement, and optimization in real time[60]. Several of the big names in open programmatic are expanding into CTV, including The Trade Desk, Xandr, Magnite, SpotX or Adform. As in display advertising, the competing DSPs differ in their access to OTT video inventory supply, targeting and optimization capabilities, measurement, reporting or brand safety features. OTT inventory, due to its current scarcity and trading issues outlined below, is typically transacted using fixed price deals, PMP deals or programmatic guaranteed rather than via open auction.

With OTT, ads are typically delivered using server-side ad insertion (SSAI). SSAI involves inserting ads directly into video content on the server side. The main advantage is providing a seamless stream of content and video for the best user experience. SSAI is often compared to client-side ad insertion (CSAI), a legacy method of stitching ads into the video stream on the side of the client (device). CSAI is on its way out, due to problems with interruptions between the video content and ads and susceptibility to ad blockers[61]. Finally, dynamic ad insertion (DAI) allows advertisers to serve different ads to individual users or households, rather than serving the same ad to everyone[62].

Current issues with connected TV

The OTT ecosystem is highly fragmented, owing to various streaming providers, operating systems, devices and naturally local data and identity regulation. Fragmentation is high both on the ecosystem as well as user level - a typical user would consume video content on multiple streaming services across several devices and platforms. Although interoperability standards are emerging to enable various technology players across the OTT supply and demand sides to achieve scale, there's still a long way to go. In the early stages of OTT growth, advertisers have overcome challenges including identity resolution, measurement, or fraud.

Given the wide gamut of devices and platforms used for video streaming today - from smart TV operating systems through game consoles to mobile phones - it is not easy to resolve identity on individual user or household level. Each platform offers different options when it comes to generating, storing and synchronizing IDs, and user duplication across broader OTT campaign is a real problem. Login-based identification seems to offer the largest potential scale, provided users are willing to sign in with stable credentials across all their devices. Such identity can not only unite the fragmented streaming device landscape, but also the technology stacks and data assets in the background. It is important to keep in mind that identity resolution always goes hand-in-hand with respecting user privacy preferences and local regulation.

An often-cited issue that stems from fragmentation and complicated identity resolution is measurement. CTV and OTT in general promises a qualitatively superior measurement standard compared to what traditional TV buyers were used to. In theory, it is possible to measure every ad impression with all the accompanying metrics (viewability, completion rate, CTR, interactions, etc.). This is way better than the panel-based reach estimates of the past. However, due to the current state of fragmentation and lack of scaled de-duplicated identity standard, precise measurement is often limited to pockets of OTT inventory operated by individual players. This should improve over time though, as common market standards develop[63]. Viewability and its measurement is a separate and important topic as well, as CTV/OTT audiences and devices sometimes behave differently to recipients of standard display advertising. For example, a screen might be off while contents and ads play, or viewers might quickly drop out when ads begin to play[64].

Fraud is a common teething problem in the programmatic ecosystem, as the various inventories and supply channels mature. Given the premium nature of OTT and CTV, the relatively high CPMs driven by advertiser demand attract fraudsters. With SSAI, it is not possible to directly measure ad delivery, and it is easier to create counterfeit servers and fraudulent ad requests. An example of this is a fraud scheme called ParrotTerra uncovered by DoubleVerify, where fraudsters tricked advertisers into buying inventory that would never be seen by real people using SSAI[65].

Many of the issues CTV/OTT faces in its early programmatic phase will be resolved over time with standardization. For example, the IAB Tech Lab released guidelines for OTT app identification to increase supply transparency[66]. As for measurement, the IAB has deprecated its legacy Video Player Ad Interface Definition (VPAID) standard and replaced it with Open Measurement Interface Definition (OMID), which is designed to support

CTV and OTT environments[67]. The OpenRTB standards are also periodically updated to support CTV[68].

Retail media

Retail media (also referred to as retail media networks) is an emerging channel currently experiencing rapid growth. In the context of programmatic, retail media is a broad term encompassing advertising that is sold both on digital retail inventory as well as inventory beyond retail sites that is owned or rented by retailers.

Several factors are contributing to the growing prominence of retail media. Perhaps most obvious and important of all is the shift of consumer spending to digital retail, boosted by COVID-19 pandemic. Just like in the offline world of brick-and-mortar stores, it is natural to try and influence consumers as close to the purchase decision as possible. While in-store shopper marketing budgets could secure attractive shelf placement or a unique display stand, in the world of digital retail media advertisers can purchase highly visible sponsored ads, prominent placements or attractive display ads. Advertisers also want to take advantage of the wealth of first-party data retailers have on their customers. In the context of the looming end of third-party cookies, closed advertising ecosystems offer a way of retaining high ROI and advertising efficiency. Retail media is particularly well positioned here, with the entire feedback loop from impression to conversion accurately measurable. On the supply side, retailers welcome and fuel the rise of retail media as a way to improve their profit margins and grow shopper marketing revenue.

Some of the best-known retail media offerings include Amazon Advertising, Walmart Connect or Target Roundel. Many smaller or regional retailers and platforms have their own solutions as well, including Best Buy, Kroger, Tesco or Instacart. While the larger retailers tend to prefer proprietary technology, players with smaller scale often rely on open programmatic solutions from the likes of The Trade Desk, Index Exchange or Criteo[69]. It remains to be seen to what extent will retail media become part of the open programmatic ecosystem.

Programmatic audio

Digital audio has been capturing an increasing share of user attention over the recent years. This trend is fueled by growing ubiquity of enabling technology including smartphones, smart watches, wireless headphones, smart speakers, connected cars or better and faster internet connectivity. Unlike more visual channels, digital audio can conveniently fit into activities unrelated to media consumption itself, such as exercise, cooking or driving. Attractive audio formats including podcasts, on-demand streaming or audiobooks further boost fast growth of digital audio.

Digital audio can be defined as any online audio listening, that is IP delivered and can be streamed or downloaded, on any device[70]. This includes online versions of broadcast AM/FM radio stations or purely online radio stations, streamed audio content, or audio on-demand. When it comes to audio ad serving, specifications are covered under VAST alongside video[71]. Some of the issues related to programmatic audio advertising include fragmentation, lack of common measurement standards or the integration of programmatic itself.

Programmatic out-of-home

Another area where programmatic ad trading is gradually (albeit more slowly compared to other channels) making progress is digital out-of-home (DOOH). Digital screens in public places, such as shopping malls, transportation hubs, stadiums, or gyms can be used to reach hundreds of people simultaneously in an automated fashion. Ads can not only be precisely targeted in terms of location, time, traffic data or weather but can also include an element of interactivity using touch screens, gestures, augmented reality or social media engagement[72].

Unlike programmatic display, where each impression is traded individually, DOOH impressions are traded in bundles on an impression/play basis or CPM conversion taking into account a screen's current audience size estimate. Digital out-of-home is closely linked to location data collected from devices like smartphones or in-store beacons. Some of the challenges are similar to other emerging channels, including unfamiliarity, fragmentation or lack of ad serving and measurement standardization[73].

About the author

Dominik Kosorin is a digital advertising professional with broad experience across the industry including Adform, Seznam.cz or Czech Publisher Exchange. He is the author of Data in Digital Advertising, as well as the well-regarded first edition of this book. He lives in Prague with an amazing wife and two incredible sons.

References

1. Schuh, Justin. „Building a more private web: A path towards making third party cookies obsolete." Blog.chromium.org, January 14, 2020. https://blog.chromium.org/2020/01/building-more-private-web-path-towards.html

2. Statcounter. "Browser Market Share Worldwide." Gs.statcounter.com, Accessed May 2022. https://gs.statcounter.com/browser-market-share#monthly-202205-202205-bar

3. Statcounter. "Desktop vs Mobile vs Tablet Market Share Worldwide." Gs.statcounter.com, Accessed May 2022. https://gs.statcounter.com/platform-market-share/desktop-mobile-tablet/worldwide/#monthly-202205-202205-bar

4. Statcounter. "Browser Market Share in Germany." Gs.statcounter.com, Accessed May 2022. https://gs.statcounter.com/browser-market-share/all/germany#monthly-202205-202205-bar

5. Statcounter. "Browser Market Share in United States Of America." Gs.statcounter.com, Accessed May 2022. https://gs.statcounter.com/browser-market-share/all/united-states-of-america#monthly-202205-202205-bar

6. Schuh, Justin. „Building a more private web: A path towards making third party cookies obsolete." Blog.chromium.org, January 14, 2020. https://blog.chromium.org/2020/01/building-more-private-web-path-towards.html

7. IAB Tech Lab. "HTML5 For Digital Advertising." https://labtechlab.com/standards/html-5/

8. Interactive Advertising Bureau. "IAB New Ad Portfolio: Advertising Creative Guidelines." https://www.iab.com/newadportfolio/

9. Kosorin, Dominik. Data in Digital Advertising: Understand the Data Landscape and Design a Winning Strategy. Milton Keynes, United Kingdom, 2018.

10. Kosorin, Dominik. Data in Digital Advertising: Understand the Data Landscape and Design a Winning Strategy. Milton Keynes, United Kingdom, 2018.

11. Interactive Advertising Bureau. https://www.iab.com/

12. Trustworthy Accountability Group. https://www.tagtoday.net/

13. Media Rating Council. http://mediaratingcouncil.org/

14. Federal Trade Commission. https://www.ftc.gov/

REFERENCES

15 Interactive Advertising Bureau. "Programmatic and automation – the publisher's perspective." https://www.iab.com/wp-content/uploads/2015/06/IAB_Digital_Simplified_Programmatic_Sept_2013.pdf

16 IAB Tech Lab. "OpenRTB (Real-Time Bidding)." https://www.iab.com/guidelines/openrtb/

17 IAB Tech Lab. "OpenRTB Version 2.6." https://iabtechlab.com/wp-content/uploads/2022/04/OpenRTB-2-6_FINAL.pdf

18 IAB Tech Lab. "OpenRTB Version 2.6." https://iabtechlab.com/wp-content/uploads/2022/04/OpenRTB-2-6_FINAL.pdf

19 IAB Tech Lab. "Open Direct 2.0 Ready For Adoption (Blog Post)." https://iabtechlab.com/standards/opendirect/

20 IAB Tech Lab. "Standards." https://iabtechlab.com/standards/

21 IAB Tech Lab. "Ads.Txt – Authorized Digital Sellers." https://iabtechlab.com/ads-txt/

22 IAB Tech Lab. "Sellers.Json." https://iabtechlab.com/sellers-json/

23 IAB Tech Lab. "Digital Video Ad Serving Template (VAST)." https://iabtechlab.com/standards/vast/

24 IAB Tech Lab. Open Measurement SDK." https://iabtechlab.com/standards/open-measurement-sdk/

25 Zawadziński, Maciej. "How Do First-Price and Second-Price Auctions Work in Online Advertising?" Clearcode.cc, August 12, 2021. https://clearcode.cc/blog/first-price-second-price-auction/#Why-the-transition-from-first-to-second-price-auctions

26 IAB Europe. "The IAB Europe guide to supply path optimization." Iabeurope.eu, September 2020. https://iabeurope.eu/wp-content/uploads/2020/09/IAB-Europe-Guide-to-SPO-Sept-2020-2.pdf

27 Zhou, Wenda. "It's Time To Zero In On Demand-Path Optimization." Adexchanger.com, November 11, 2020. https://www.adexchanger.com/the-sell-sider/its-time-to-zero-in-on-demand-path-optimization/

28 Paparo, Ari. "The Strategic Implications Of Header Bidding." AdExchanger.com, October 23, 2015. http://adexchanger.com/the-sell-sider/the-strategic-implications-of-header-bidding/

29 Trustworthy Accountability Group. https://www.tagtoday.net/

30 IAB Tech Lab. "Ads.Txt – Authorized Digital Sellers." https://iabtechlab.com/ads-txt/

31 IAB Tech Lab. "Sellers.Json." https://iabtechlab.com/sellers-json/

32 Kosorin, Dominik. Data in Digital Advertising: Understand the Data Landscape and Design a Winning Strategy. Milton Keynes, United Kingdom, 2018.

33 Kosorin, Dominik. Data in Digital Advertising: Understand the Data Landscape and Design a Winning Strategy. Milton Keynes, United Kingdom, 2018.

34 Kosorin, Dominik. Data in Digital Advertising: Understand the Data Landscape and Design a Winning Strategy. Milton Keynes, United Kingdom, 2018.

35 Kosorin, Dominik. Data in Digital Advertising: Understand the Data Landscape and Design a Winning Strategy. Milton Keynes, United Kingdom, 2018.

36 Buchheim, Dennis; Shetty, Amit. "Demystifying identifiers and understanding their critical roles in advertising." Iabtechlab.com, March 19, 2018. https://iabtechlab.com/blog/demystifying-identifiers-and-understanding-their-critical-roles-in-advertising/

37 Information Commissioner's Office. "GDPR Key definitions." Ico.org.uk, Accessed November 2017. https://ico.org.uk/for-organisations/guide-to-the-general-data-protection-regulation-gdpr/key-definitions

38 IAB Europe GDPR Implementation Working Group. "GDPR Compliance Primer." Iabeurope.eu, May 22, 2017. https://www.iabeurope.eu/wp-content/uploads/2017/06/20172205-IA-BEU-GIG-Working-Paper01_GDPR-Compliance-Primer.pdf

39 IAB Europe GDPR Implementation Working Group. "GDPR Compliance Primer." Iabeurope.eu, May 22, 2017. https://www.iabeurope.eu/wp-content/uploads/2017/06/20172205-IA-BEU-GIG-Working-Paper01_GDPR-Compliance-Primer.pdf

40 IAB Europe GDPR Implementation Working Group. "GDPR Compliance Primer." Iabeurope.eu, May 22, 2017. https://www.iabeurope.eu/wp-content/uploads/2017/06/20172205-IA-BEU-GIG-Working-Paper01_GDPR-Compliance-Primer.pdf

41 IAB Europe. "TCF – Transparency & Consent Framework." https://iabeurope.eu/transparency-consent-framework/

42 IAB Europe. "CMP List." https://iabeurope.eu/cmp-list/

43 IAB Tech Lab. "Transparency and Consent String with Global Vendor & CMP List Formats." Github.com, Accessed May 2022. https://github.com/InteractiveAdvertisingBureau/GDPR-Transparency-and-Consent-Framework/blob/master/TCFv2/IAB%20Tech%20Lab%20-%20Consent%20string%20and%20vendor%20list%20formats%20v2.md

REFERENCES

44 Skiera, Bernd et al. The Impact of the General Data Protection Regulation (GDPR) on the Online Advertising Market. Bernd Skiera, 2022.

45 State of California Department of Justice. "California Consumer Privacy Act (CCPA)." Oag.ca.gov, Accessed April 2022. https://oag.ca.gov/privacy/ccpa

46 Consumer Federation of California. "California Online Privacy Protection Act (CalOPPA)." Consumercal.org, July 29, 2015. https://consumercal.org/about-cfc/cfc-education-foundation/california-online-privacy-protection-act-caloppa-3

47 Interactive Advertising Bureau. "Digital Advertising Regulation 101." Iab.com, February 3, 2014. https://www.iab.com/news/digital-advertising-regulation-101

48 Consumer Federation of California. "California Online Privacy Protection Act (CalOPPA)." Consumercal.org, July 29, 2015. https://consumercal.org/about-cfc/cfc-education-foundation/california-online-privacy-protection-act-caloppa-3

49 Interactive Advertising Bureau. "Digital Advertising Regulation 101." Iab.com, February 3, 2014. https://www.iab.com/news/digital-advertising-regulation-101

50 Interactive Advertising Bureau. "Digital Advertising Regulation 101." Iab.com, February 3, 2014. https://www.iab.com/news/digital-advertising-regulation-101

51 IAB.com. "Self-Regulatory Program for Online Behavioral Advertising." https://www.iab.com/news/self-regulatory-program-for-online-behavioral-advertising/

52 Digital Advertising Alliance. http://digitaladvertisingalliance.org

53 Digital Advertising Alliance. "DAA Self-Regulatory Principles." Digitaladvertisingalliance.org. http://digitaladvertisingalliance.org/principles

54 YourAdChoices. http://youradchoices.com

55 Disconnect, Inc. "Disconnect-tracking-protection." Github.com, Accessed April 2022. https://github.com/disconnectme/disconnect-tracking-protection

56 Google Developers. "Privacy Sandbox on Android." https://developer.android.com/design-for-safety/ads

57 IAB Europe. "The IAB Europe guide to the programmatic CTV opportunity in Europe." Iabeurope.eu, April 2021. https://iabeurope.eu/wp-content/uploads/2021/04/IAB-Europe-Guide-to-the-Programmatic-CTV-Opportunity-in-Europe_April_2021.pdf

58 Media Rating Council. "Server-Side Ad Insertion and OTT Guidance." Mediaratingcouncil.org, August 2021. http://www.mediaratingcouncil.org/083021%20SSAI%20and%20OTT%20Guidance%20%20FINAL.pdf

59. Media Rating Council. "Server-Side Ad Insertion and OTT Guidance." Mediaratingcouncil.org, August 2021. http://www.mediaratingcouncil.org/083021%20SSAI%20and%20OTT%20Guidance%20%20FINAL.pdf

60. IAB Europe. "The IAB Europe guide to the programmatic CTV opportunity in Europe." iabeurope.eu, April 2021. https://iabeurope.eu/wp-content/uploads/2021/04/IAB-Europe-Guide-to-the-Programmatic-CTV-Opportunity-in-Europe_April_2021.pdf

61. Sweeney, Michael; Zawiślak, Paulina. "What Is Connected TV (CTV) & OTT Advertising and How Does It Work? [infographic]." Clearcode.cc, May 4, 2022. https://clearcode.cc/blog/ctv-ott-infographic/

62. IAB Europe. "The IAB Europe guide to the programmatic CTV opportunity in Europe." iabeurope.eu, April 2021. https://iabeurope.eu/wp-content/uploads/2021/04/IAB-Europe-Guide-to-the-Programmatic-CTV-Opportunity-in-Europe_April_2021.pdf

63. IAB Tech Lab. "OpenRTB (Real-Time Bidding)." https://www.iab.com/guidelines/openrtb/

64. IAB Europe. "The IAB Europe guide to the programmatic CTV opportunity in Europe." iabeurope.eu, April 2021. https://iabeurope.eu/wp-content/uploads/2021/04/IAB-Europe-Guide-to-the-Programmatic-CTV-Opportunity-in-Europe_April_2021.pdf

65. IAB Europe. "The IAB Europe guide to the programmatic CTV opportunity in Europe." iabeurope.eu, April 2021. https://iabeurope.eu/wp-content/uploads/2021/04/IAB-Europe-Guide-to-the-Programmatic-CTV-Opportunity-in-Europe_April_2021.pdf

66. IAB Tech Lab. "IAB Tech Lab OTT/CTV Store Assigned App Identification Guidelines." iabtechlab.com, December 2019. https://iabtechlab.com/wp-content/uploads/2020/08/IAB-Tech-Lab-OTT-store-assigned-App-Identification-Guidelines-2020.pdf

67. IAB Tech Lab. "Video Player-Ad Interface Definition (VPAID)" https://iabtechlab.com/standards/video-player-ad-interface-definition-vpaid/

68. IAB Tech Lab. "OpenRTB (Real-Time Bidding)." https://www.iab.com/guidelines/openrtb/

69. Hercher, James. "How Retail Media Ad Platforms Are Rewriting The Walled Garden Playbook." Adexchanger.com, April 27, 2022. https://www.adexchanger.com/ecommerce-2/how-retail-media-ad-platforms-are-rewriting-the-walled-garden-playbook/

70. IAB Europe. "The buyer's guide to digital audio." iabeurope.eu, November 2020. https://iabeurope.eu/wp-content/uploads/2020/11/Buyers-Guide-to-Digital-Audio-IAB-Europe-Nov-2020.pdf

REFERENCES

71 IAB Tech Lab. "Digital Video Ad Serving Template (VAST)." https://iabtechlab.com/standards/vast/

72 IAB Europe. "IAB Europe navigator: Programmatic out of home advertising." Iabeurope.com, November 2020. https://iabeurope.eu/wp-content/uploads/2021/10/IAB-Europe-Navigator-Programatic-OOH-Nov-2020-v2.pdf

73 IAB Europe. "IAB Europe navigator: Programmatic out of home advertising." Iabeurope.com, November 2020. https://iabeurope.eu/wp-content/uploads/2021/10/IAB-Europe-Navigator-Programatic-OOH-Nov-2020-v2.pdf

Email: dominik.kosorin@adtechresearch.com
LinkedIn: www.linkedin.com/in/dominikkosorin

www.ingramcontent.com/pod-product-compliance
Lightning Source LLC
LaVergne TN
LVHW041947070526
838199LV00051BA/2930